PREACHI
HISTOR

MOWBRAY PREACHING SERIES

Series Editor: D. W. Cleverley Ford

Preaching the Risen Christ: D. W. Cleverley Ford
Preaching through the Acts of the Apostles: D. W. Cleverley Ford
Preaching through the Prophets: John B. Taylor
More Preaching from the New Testament: D. W. Cleverley Ford
Preaching on Devotional Occasions: D. W. Cleverley Ford
More Preaching on Favourite Hymns: Frank Colquhoun
Preaching on Special Occasions, Volume 3: Edward H. Patey
Preaching on Great Themes: D. W. Cleverley Ford
Preaching on the Holy Spirit: D. W. Cleverley Ford
Preaching on the Lord's Supper: Encounter with Christ: Ian MacLeod
Preaching on Prayer: Monica Ditmas
Preaching on the Incarnate Christ: D. W. Cleverley Ford
Preaching for Our Planet: Hugh Montefiore
Preaching on the Crucifixion: D. W. Cleverley Ford
Preaching for All Seasons: John Vipond
Preaching on the Historical Jesus: D. W. Cleverley Ford

Preaching at the Parish Communion:
  ASB Epistles – Sundays: Year One, Volume 2: Dennis Runcorn
  ASB Gospels – Sundays: Year One: Dennis Runcorn
  ASB Gospels – Sundays: Year One, Volume 2: Eric Devenport
  ASB Gospels – Sundays: Year Two, Volume 2: Peter Morris

PREACHING ON THE HISTORICAL JESUS

D.W. CLEVERLEY FORD

MOWBRAY

Mowbray
A Cassell imprint
Villiers House, 41/47 Strand,
London WC2N 5JE

First published 1993

British Library Cataloguing-in-Publication Data
A catalogue record for this book is available from the British Library.

ISBN 0-264-67305-0

Typeset by Colset Pte Ltd, Singapore
Printed and bound in Great Britain by
Biddles Ltd, Guildford and King's Lynn

CONTENTS

ACKNOWLEDGEMENTS

I am grateful to Ruth McCurry, Religious Editor of Cassell, the publishers, for her comments on the text of this book while it was in the process of being written; also to Barbara Hodge at Canterbury for her expertise in converting yet another of my MSS into a perfect typescript and meeting the publication deadline.

The following books have stimulated my thinking on the historical Jesus:

A. B. Bruce, *The Training of the Twelve* (T. & T. Clark, 1898)

Edward Schillebeeckx, *Jesus* (Collins, 1979)

Morna Hooker, *The Message of Mark* (Epworth Press, 1983)

J. L. Houlden, *Jesus: A Question of Identity* (SPCK, 1992)

H. M. Kuitert, *I Have My Doubts* (SCM Press, 1993)

N. T. Wright, *Who Was Jesus?* (SPCK, 2nd impression 1993)

in addition to the standard commentaries on the English and Greek texts of the New Testament gospels.

D. W. CLEVERLEY FORD
Lingfield 1993

INTRODUCTION

In my book *Preaching on Great Themes* (Mowbray, 1989) I included a sermon entitled 'Who is Jesus?' making the point that the identity of Jesus cannot be known simply by a process of historical research however scientifically conducted. Jesus has to be encountered existentially, that is to say we must know the Christ of experience first. This may come in various ways the most prominent of which will probably be through fellowship of the Christian community. Here the Spirit of Christ, who is the Holy Spirit, is *caught*. This experience is initial and basic. For any degree of Christian maturity however, there must be acquaintance with the historical Jesus, what he did, what he said and the impression he made, and no doubt in the modern world some of the critical questions involved. One of the ways of accomplishing this is through preaching. To encourage this and to help in this is the purpose of this book.

Jesus is of course an historical figure and therefore to some extent culturally conditioned but he is also strikingly contemporary. He was nothing if not arresting in speech, action and, no doubt, in personal presence. He was a charismatic individual. But he was and is elusive, and not only that but disconcerting, and yet with it all compassionate and very strong. The historical Jesus cannot be left out. He is the heart and soul of Christianity, and if he is replaced with dogma be it never so orthodox, or a radicalism be it never so unorthodox, or by a system of moral values no doubt essential for the welfare of the community, it will not lay hold of more than a tiny proportion of mankind. The historical Jesus is Christianity's supreme and indispensable asset. For centuries he has never failed to intrigue an extraordinary diversity of people, which fact alone surely calls for a strategy in preaching that imaginatively presents this man in such a way as to generate interest, questioning, and it is to be hoped even belief.

It is not possible to offer a life of Jesus. Not only are comprehensive resource materials lacking but those we possess in the New Testament may to some extent be coloured by what the early Church came to believe about him. The recognition of this must not however be pressed too far. That the titles 'Lord' and 'Christ' given to Jesus occur rarely in the gospels, and that in the synoptic gospels there is almost no mention of the Holy Spirit is testimony to the care with which the writers sought to portray *the man they knew*. And no follower of Jesus would have invented the story of what happened in the garden of Gethsemane, nor have disclosed the miserable misunderstanding of the twelve disciples unless these things were true. A proper conservatism is not without support therefore in our critical handling of the material with which to present a picture of this man.

I have used the word 'picture'. It is a *picture* of Jesus that needs to be presented in preaching. It is a picture or rather a series of pictures that I have risked trying to sketch in this book. I see the four gospels, yes, even to some extent including the fourth gospel, as placing before us impressionist drawings of Jesus in action. There is a similarity between them and the sketches that used to reach us from the wartime artists on the battle front before the advent of the modern camera. No doubt they were partly interpretative but they were not idiosyncratic, there was an authenticity about them. From them we did gain a true impression of what it was like to be a soldier in the battle line, the men we saw were real men and their actions and reactions were not the product of imagination. Now the gospel writers do not supply us with drawings, their pictures are word pictures presented with a supreme economy of line. The gospels could almost be described as a collection of vivid short stories about Jesus. This word 'story' needs to be emphasized. The preaching of the Christian gospel as it is presented to us in the New Testament begins with *the story* of Jesus of Nazareth, not with elaborated doctrine. It begins with an exhibition of word pictures of this man in action leaving us to make our own judgement about him. This surely is a beginning which preaching ought never to leave behind.

There is a problem here. How far is the use of imagination legitimate in representing the gospel stories in preaching? Imagination must play its part. No artist, no writer will succeed who does not draft his material imaginatively. If he is to catch the attention of those who come to encounter his work, and if it is to make an impression, perhaps lasting, he must pay attention to presentation. The contributory parts of the picture/story are not merely to be thrown together. There must be purposeful arrangement evident in the focus point or climax. And were not the gospel writers aware of this basic principle? And was not preaching behind the writing?

Is not this the reason why the stories display a distinctive *form* as those who have studied form criticism are aware? Clearly they were imaginatively shaped to produce an impression of Jesus. The overriding purpose was not to draw up a comprehensive record accurate down to the last detail, which is not to say the stories are inaccurate, but to answer the question: what sort of man was this? See for example Mark 4.41. When, therefore, the historical Jesus is preached, this is the question that must control the presentation and for which the use of imagination will be necessary, albeit disciplined imagination, imagination that does not sit loosely to scholarship. It will be argued that each writer/preacher will present 'his own Jesus'. There is some truth in this but the overriding question is: as a result of the presentation, imperfect as it is, can those who encounter it receive an authentic impression of this man?

And let not the situation of those who hear/see the presentation be forgotten. They will not be sitting in an academic lecture room but people who on Monday morning will be occupying a desk, operating machine tools, scanning the shelves at the supermarket, feeding hungry mouths. The presentation must have the ordinary people of the community in mind. I hope my book does not fall down at this point.

D.W.C.F.
1993

1

JESUS WITH A FACE

You need only say the word and the boy will be cured.

MATTHEW 8.8 (NEB)

I am going to preach about the historical Jesus, that is, the Jesus
who walked about in Judaea and Galilee. I am not going to enlarge
on the Christ of the Creeds—'very God of very God, begotten not
made, being of one substance with the Father by whom all things
were made'—though I assent to those Creeds. Neither do I intend
theologizing on the mystery of his Person, and it is a mystery, the
Godhead and Manhood in Jesus, though there is proper place for
this enquiry but not in a sermon. What I shall attempt to present
is Jesus with a face. I shall attempt this because, necessary as
theological presentations have been, especially in the early centuries
of the Christian Church (and they still are important), they leave
us with a faceless Jesus which to some extent is what many people
feel St Paul in his letters has given us. This is not what the gospels
display, they present a recognizable person to whom we can relate
either with warmth or disapproval, anything but an abstraction
though not without mystery.

1 OUR KNOWLEDGE ABOUT JESUS

Perhaps you reckon I shall be wasting your time and mine. We all
know about Jesus of Nazareth. But are you sure? Yes, of course his
name is familiar, and books about him have never ceased to flow
from the printing presses and not all written by Christians. Jesus
intrigues people, there is scarcely any more familiar name. It would
be futile for anyone to attempt to produce a history of the world
and to leave Jesus out, but what do most of us know about him?
What about Church people? We take him for granted. He is part
of our mental furniture placed there in our upbringing (I speak for
myself), baby Jesus in the manger at Christmas. Jesus, the cuddly

1

little boy, Jesus the kindly man who took children into his arms; for many people never much else *except* the Christ of the crucifix carved in wood or stone or painted on canvas, standing there as a terrible reminder of our cruel world. Or at another extreme Christ is presented as the Saviour in evangelistic campaigns calling for decisions for Christ, or the mysterious presence in the sacrament; but what do we know of the historical Jesus, Jesus with a face?

Maybe you say to me: but what are we able to know of him?— the real Jesus, as some would express the question. There are no photographs of him, no portraits, no sketches. This is true but there are the word pictures, the stories about him in the New Testament gospels from which we can gather how people who actually encountered him and saw him. Critics exist, I know, who reject this material on the grounds that it is so 'touched up', even 'blown up', especially in the miracle stories, by writers with an axe to grind that it is wholly unreliable. This is a fantastic assertion. Admittedly these stories cannot be read as bare history, some would say as factual history, but is there such a thing? Always a measure of interepretation enters in any telling of what has happened; what is included and what is omitted, is an interpretation of what is important in the view of the one who does the telling. So with the gospel stories, but the picture they present is not faked, it is not imaginary, its originality is too great for this to be possible. We can reliably know something of what the historical Jesus was like, we can, as it were, see Jesus with a face.

2 WHY ENQUIRE ABOUT THE HISTORICAL JESUS?

But why should anyone want to know about Jesus? I have already hinted at one simple answer—because he has become and is one of the most famous figures in world history. Suppose however we are not particularly interested in history, after all Jesus lived in Galilee and Judaea two thousand years ago. We are not for the most part historians. But Jesus is not simply an historical figure, he is at the heart of our religion and is therefore connected to us at the deepest point of our personal existence, our fears, our hopes, our regrets and our aspirations. Religion exists, persists, because we feel the need of a power outside ourselves in an uncertain world, and an untried future, and Jesus embodies that power. This is why we wish to know about him. We wish to know what manner of a person he was to accomplish this for us. We wish, as it were, to see his face.

2

I am very anxious to stress at the outset this religious point at which we begin our enquiry into the historical Jesus. He is, first of all, our Lord and Christ, our Saviour, our Redeemer, our Friend, our Teacher, our King . . . there are a dozen titles and more given him in the New Testament. We do not set out as neutral secular historians. I must add this: I do not see the significance of Jesus only in what he said and not in what he was, that is, in his person, although this is a modern trend. Repeatedly I shall ask in these sermons, Who is this man with this face? What kind of person is he?

To answer this question, or if I may be more specific, to enable you to formulate your own answer, which is much more important, I shall present to you, or rather *re*-present to you some word pictures we are given in the gospel stories; at least I shall begin there because the New Testament begins there. Surprisingly the first gospel, St Mark, that is, the first to be written, opens with the words 'Here begins the Gospel of Jesus Christ the Son of God' and then proceeds in chapter after chapter to tell stories about him in which we can see his face. Apparently, to proclaim the gospel this is what has to be done. In telling the story of the historical Jesus in these sermons therefore I make the claim that I shall be preaching the gospel of Jesus Christ. At the outset I shall draw mainly on the first three gospels, the Synoptic gospels as they are called, because they all, though with different emphases and viewpoints, tell the same story as far as the outline is concerned. But I shall not forget the fourth gospel, which is different for it combines history and theological reflections on the Person of Jesus. For example, it begins by calling him the *Word made flesh*, the Jesus of whom it tells is God incarnate.

Now it may be that someone is thinking that in preaching the historical Jesus, Jesus with a face, I am missing out on the heart of the gospel which is not what he said or did but why and how he died, indeed the death on the cross which Easter celebrates. But I shall not miss this out. In any case it is not possible to present a comprehensive story of the life of anyone without telling how that person died. I go further. Jesus sensed from his earliest days in his ministry when he began to proclaim the Kingdom of God that he would pay with his life for that proclamtion. He faced (note the word) this from the very start. All the same he went on teaching till the very end, but what we have to decide is whether we can stop short at respecting him as a superb, even unique teacher.

I shall not undervalue the teaching of Jesus although I do not count it as the centre of his ministry. Jesus was a prophet certainly. The people of his day were quick to categorize him as a prophet and they were not wrong. But that is not the ultimate estimate of

Jesus, it is not in the last resort why we hang upon his words. We have come to believe that in his words we hear the word of God. Our Christian belief is that in encountering Jesus, yes with a human face, we are encountering God. This is why his teaching is unique. This is why in our deliberations and dilemmas we turn to the gospels to discover what Jesus said, and after we have read it, a sense of finality takes hold of us. So I bid you not only to see the historical Jesus, Jesus with a face, but also to hear him, and I think you will hear him more readily if you have seen him.

3 THE CENTURION

I have to some extent been talking theoretically though not I hope in technical jargon. It is time for me to end with a story as an illustration of the procedure I shall follow in these sermons on the historical Jesus. I have lifted it out of St Matthew's gospel and it concerns a soldier, captain of a hundred men, technically called a centurion. There were sixty of these in every Roman legion of six thousand men. They were tough, indeed rough. Their job militarily was not spectacular, it was to maintain the discipline of the troops, and they were reckoned to be the backbone of the army. They carried a vine stick (Latin *vitis*), the symbol of their office, and used it frequently on their men. They tended to be laughed at for their hobnailed shoes, their thick calves and their generally unkempt roughness but they were thoughtful and thoroughly reliable. One such was based at Capernaum which Jesus had chosen as the base of his ministry in Galilee. He occupied a house outside the town itself. Jesus and this Roman soldier knew each other and came into close contact when the soldier was desperate for his boy at home paralysed and racked with pain. He asked Jesus for help. The response was immediate, not 'I will see what I can do', but 'I will come and heal him'. It meant for Jesus a walk of a mile or more during which time the centurion got cold feet, as we say, not simply about whether Jesus, a Jew, would cross the threshold of a gentile; but *ought* he even to ask him? 'Sir, who am I to have you under my roof? You need only say the word and the boy will be cured.' Leave aside for the moment his implicit respect for Jesus in addressing him as 'Sir' (Greek *Kurie*), acknowledging the gap between them. Leave aside, too, his confidence that Jesus would heal his boy and the love of this rough soldier for him, and concentrate on how he continued his appeal. It tells us how he saw Jesus. 'You need only

4

say the word and the boy will be cured. I know for I am myself under orders with soldiers under me. I say to one, "Go" and he goes; to another "Come here" and he comes; and to my servant "Do this" and he does it.' Clearly this centurion had been watching Jesus for weeks, perhaps months and had come to the conclusion that here was someone who could command. Jesus was in fact like himself. Astonishing thought but not to be denied. The centurion saw Jesus as exuding authority and power though he wore no hobnailed shoes and carried no vine stick. Jesus was worth approaching on behalf of his boy because clearly what he ordered would come to pass. He was that sort of person.

So I ask my question, what was the historical Jesus like, Jesus with a face? Can we know? This soldier clearly knew. Jesus was like himself in the matter of obvious personal authority. When he commanded you had to obey. He was like that. This is what my text for today epitomizes the word of the centurion to Jesus, Matthew 8, verse 8: 'You need only say the word and the boy will be cured.'

2

AN AUTHORITATIVE PREACHER

*The people were astounded at his teaching, for, unlike the doctors of
the law, he taught with a note of authority.*

MARK 1.22

When I was a student in London I used to make my way on some
Friday evenings to hear the celebrated Bible expositor Dr Campbell
Morgan conduct a short service of worship in Buckingham Gate
Congregational Church, Westminster, the focal point of which was
his exposition of a passage of Scripture. The place was packed, hundreds of people, rapt in close attention. What I recall after all these
years is seeing this striking white-haired man with a strong face
climb the stairs up on to the dais and stand at the lectern at which
he would preach; and when the service was over return by the same
stairs to disappear through a door at the back, presumably to the
vestry. I never saw him more closely than that, never spoke to him,
never shook his hand. I saw him and I heard him, that was all, but
I was impressed, all because of the quality of his preaching on that
platform which could scarcely be called a pulpit.

1 AN IMPRESSIVE PREACHER

The public of Jesus' time first encountered him as a preacher and
was astonished by his authority. This reaction was crystallized one
Sabbath day in Capernaum when he arrived in the synagogue, not
alone but accompanied by four men whom they knew as fishermen
on the lake, but not now. They had abandoned this means of
livelihood at this preacher's command simply to be with him. And
there he was making for the place in the synagogue where the Scripture was accustomed to be read and the sermon preached. The congregation's attention was minimal. Sermons were invariably boring.
Once again the hearers would yawn, fidget and whisper to their
neihbours behind cupped hands. None of this however happened.
Instead astonishment. They had never witnessed such preaching. It

6

was strong, clear and above all authoritative. The hearers were gripped. It was the authority that gripped them, the personal authority of the man in the preacher's seat. He did not laboriously quote from learned authorities, he spoke on his own authority. It was the man and everything about the man that astonished the worshippers in the synagogue that Sabbath day in Capernaum.

And while he was preaching there came an interruption that deepened that amazement into awe of him. A poor demented creature in the congregation, overcome by the almost uncanny tension created by the intensity of the corporate listening, shrieked out 'What do you want with us, Jesus of Nazareth? Have you come to destroy us? I know who you are – the Holy One of God.' But the preacher was having no interference with his authority. Peremptorily he ordered the man be silent and his hostile spirit be gone, both of which at once occurred but not without further convulsions and shouting. And when the service was over all Capernaum was talking about what had happened in the synagogue, and not only in Capernaum but throughout the whole district. Here was an authoritative figure who would suffer no resistance to his authority. This was Jesus of Nazareth. Everything about him spoke of authority.

2 THE CLASH OF AUTHORITIES

But the religious authorities were uneasy. Even Jerusalem was alerted. They sensed a challenge to their position developing in Galilee, notably in Capernaum. And so investigators infiltrated the crowds listening to Jesus' teaching. They were on the lookout for incriminating evidence, and one day they hit on what they half expected. All 'innocent like' they were sitting in the packed room of a house, possibly Peter's down by the lake, with a great crowd standing around the door eager to listen to Jesus. Completely unexpected there was a scuffle on the roof, a large hole appeared through which a man on a mattress was being lowered before Jesus, clearly a paralytic hopeful of healing. Without more ado, and with the kindly words 'My son', Jesus said 'your sins are forgiven'. Did knowing nods pass between the spies sitting there? Their suspicions were justified. This Jesus was a blasphemer. Who but God alone can forgive sins? Now they would indeed have something to report back to Jerusalem even if they did need to soft pedal the sequence of the paralytic standing up at Jesus' command, picking up his mattress and going home.

Soon after, far from letting the conflict settle Jesus goaded his opponents still further with his attitude to sinners. Down by the lake there sat one called Levi son of Alphaeus in his little office collecting customs dues, a notorious collaborator with the country's enemies, hated by everybody. Jesus called him to follow him and he did, he became a disciple. And worse than that, to celebrate the event Levi gave a great party which his tax-gatherer friends and Jesus attended. People saw him sitting there with that riff-raff. And if the religious authorities' spies did not actually see him they certainly heard all about this scandalous reception as Jesus intended they should. He had gone over to the attack. Levi was deliberately chosen at the opening of his ministry to make clear to all who had eyes to see what his attitude to sinners was to be, anything but exclusion, without more ado. He faced the conflict that would arise head on, he even instigated it.

There was more to come. Anyone on the lookout for further instances of the battle between the authority of Jesus and the hostilities of the religious authorities did not need to look very far. There was the day when all with any respect for the proprieties of piety were fasting, but not Jesus nor his disciples. And another day when he with his disciples were making their way through the cornfields plucking the ears of corn and eating them as they went, he did not stop them because it was the Sabbath and technically they were breaking it. His reply to the charge of his opponents was that the Sabbath was made for the sake of man and not man for the Sabbath.

The real crunch however came on another Sabbath when he attended a synagogue. There was a man with a withered arm in the congregation. Suspicious men were watching carefully to see whether or not Jesus would heal him. Had they perhaps planted the poor man there as a test case? The law had it that healing could be performed on the Sabbath if it were a matter of life and death but no one could make that assertion in the case of a withered limb! It could wait for healing till the next day. Jesus saw his chance and jumped at it. 'Come and stand out here' he authoritatively commanded the ailing man. He intended everyone should see what he was about to do. There was to be no secrecy but rather an open attack on what he saw as a ridiculous prohibition. Turning to his opponents, and with his patient (so to speak) standing before him, he asked 'Is it permitted to do good or to do evil on the Sabbath, to save life or to kill?' They had nothing to say. And then everyone in the synagogue saw what was so frequently a characteristic of Jesus, he looked round at the faces close by. People were never to

8

forget that searching glance of his. His eyes seemed to look through people. Then two apparently conflicting emotions were registered on his face, anger and sorrow all because of what he read as obstinate stupidity on the part of those whose intent it was to force the official line about Sabbath healing. He had no sympathy for unreasonableness in religion and none for those who placed the law before human need. With that authoritative manner of his he commanded the wretched public exhibit in the synagogue, his wizened limb hanging limp beside him, 'Stretch out your arm'. How ridiculous! He could not, it was atrophied, the power of his limb had dried up. He had no power. This was true so long as he looked down at his arm, but when he looked into the face of Jesus and the power there, he could. The useless limb was completely restored.

This incident marked the end of the beginning of the conflict between the authoritative Jesus and the religious authorities of his day. A council was set up how to do away with this challenger in their midst, roping in the party that was hand in glove with Herod the puppet King of Galilee and who in truth cared little for religion one way or the other. It was a clear sign of their desperation. Much water however was yet to pass under the bridge.

3 THE NATURE OF JESUS' AUTHORITY

Now we have to ask what was the nature of Jesus' authority and how did he obtain it? Certainly not from his background. Nazareth where he was reared was an intellectual and cultural backwater. Nor had he passed through the rabbinical institutions of his day and, as it were, graduated. He possessed no authorization to preach and teach and could not display or wear the insignia of authorization. He appeared as one of the people and the common people at that. So what was it?

In all the mainstream Churches of our day, and long before our day, three requirements were and are necessary for a public minister to carry out his calling. He must have a sense of a call from God, hence the use of the word 'calling' for his work. It is improper for anyone to choose to be a priest or Christian minister without being able to answer in the affirmative the question, 'Do you believe that you have a call from God?' But the call or sense of call is not by itself sufficient, there has to be a testing of it by the Church, or representative of the Church, and with it some instruction or training. This because it is possible to be deluded about a call, and

9

also because spiritual and intellectual equipment is necessary. Then thirdly there has to be authorization of the ministry by the Church or representatives of the Church: most often by a bishop.

How then does this apply to Jesus? Obviously none of it except the initial call. Jesus left the carpenter's shop in Nazareth, his call to his ministry confirmed at the Jordan river when he was empowered with the Spirit of God. So when he stood up in the Nazareth synagogue on a return visit and read the Scripture, he began 'The spirit of the Lord is upon me because he has anointed me; he has sent me to announce good news to the poor . . .' (Luke 4.18) but no one knew anything about this anointing except Jesus. His call was not examined, he was not authorized by anyone. There was however evidence of the reality of his call and of the power given him in the wonderful works of healing that characterized his ministry and the authority of his preaching. It astonished the hearers. They had never heard anything like it. So Jesus received a popular authorization of his ministry and not an official one. Therein lay the seeds of conflict and therein the reason why he was, from early on, a divisive figure and remained so till the very end.

This is still the situation with regard to him. *Proofs* about Jesus, who he was and what was the nature of his authority, are unobtainable. But how comes it that his influence it still undying in the modern world so culturally different from that which he inhabited? And how comes it that lives throughout history have been transformed by his influence, and by no means only of the weak and unintelligent? This historical Jesus has still to be reckoned with. We still have to make our own decision about him. Conflict never has been, never will be absent, as soon as he comes upon our scene of consideration. We are forced to say 'yes' or 'no' with regard to him or perhaps 'I don't know'. The 'yes' decision is the seed of faith. You ask what faith is—it is certainly more than this initial seed, it may develop into the Christ of experience, but the Jesus of history must always be kept in focus. We cannot be Christians *apart* from him.

3

WORDS AND WORKS

*Now after John was arrested, Jesus came into Galilee,
preaching the gospel of God, and saying, 'The time is fulfilled,
and the kingdom of God is at hand; repent, and believe
in the gospel.'*

MARK 1.14, 15 (RSV)

I would like you to consider, if you will, how you would respond if someone from another country approached you with the request 'Tell us about your great wartime Prime Minister, Winston Churchill. What was he like? What sort of person was he? Why was it that he became so famous, in fact one of the outstanding figures of history?' You would think hard, but you would know that it would not suffice to tell where he was born, what school he attended, what England was like when he rose to high office. You would have to make a full mention of his speeches, bringing in some of his memorable sayings like 'blood, toil, tears and sweat'. And you would have to go on and tell how the nation hung on his words in its darkest days. His speeches did something to people. Indeed you could say Churchill's speeches *were Churchill*, the authentic Churchill. They couldn't be copied, they couldn't be invented.

But he was not only a speaker, he was a man of action. And the two interlock, they always interlock in an outstanding character. His words are effective. What he does speaks, indeed actions speak louder than words. If therefore we wish to make a proper estimate of any famous historical person we must pay close attention to *his words and his works*. And this is true of the historical Jesus we have been considering in these sermons. We must pay close attention to his teaching and we must pay close attention to his wonderful works.

1 THE TEACHING OF JESUS

First then the teaching of Jesus. How did he teach? How has it come down to us in the New Testament gospels? Certainly not in the form

11

of lectures or long abstract arguments. There is nothing like a thesis. Instead there are memorable pithy sayings like 'Can the blind lead the blind, shall they not both fall into the ditch?' and 'You are the light of the world, a city set on a hill cannot be hid' and 'The labourer is worthy of his hire'. A special class of these sayings goes under the name of the Beatitudes and the Woes (see for example Luke 6): 'Blessed are the poor in spirit, for theirs is the kingdom of heaven', 'Woe unto you that are rich, for you have received your consolation', which, be it noted, is not a threat, but a sigh over a condition which can be sorrowful. Some of these sayings crop up in dialogues, perhaps in answer to a question, sometimes friendly, at other times hostile, but all apparently 'off the cuff'. There were also extended forms of teaching some of it to the crowds who flocked to hear him, some in intimate association with his twelve disciples taken aside. To the crowds he used the parable as a teaching medium, attractively simple on the surface but actually posing subtle questions which the hearers were left to puzzle over themselves. More distinctive still is the fact that a large part of the teaching of Jesus was cast into poetic form making it memorable, especially if repeated over and over again as it probably was. The basis of this poetic form was what is called 'parallelism', one line balancing another as in 'He makes his sun to rise on the evil and the good, and sends his rain on the just and the unjust'. This is the simplest form but there were also more complicated structures. All in all the range of the teaching is astonishing. And if the saying about teaching is true, 'the style is the man', it is in paying close attention to what Jesus said and how he said it that we come closest to the historical Jesus as a person. What is more it is the authentic Jesus that we encounter. And note this – the teaching style and content is too distinctive and individualistic to have been put into his mouth by subsequent writers. The words *are his* and no one else's.

But what, you may ask, was the underlying theme of his teaching? There can be no doubt. St Mark sets it out in the first page of his gospel. 'Now after John was arrested, Jesus came into Galilee, preaching the gospel of God, and saying, "The time is fulfilled, and the kingdom of God is at hand; repent, and believe in the gospel"' (Mark 1.14–15). At the back of everyone's mind was the hope that the Kingdom of God would dawn for Israel, 'then shall the lame man leap as an hart and the tongue of the dumb shall sing' (Isaiah 35.6), a time of peace and plenty when everyone would dwell securely 'under his vine and under his fig tree', and the enemies of the nation be no more. Of course people were all ears when Jesus announced this good news (the word 'gospel' means

12

good news). 'The time is fulfilled, the Kingdom of God is at hand', and if the dawn of this new day required repentance and belief in this gospel well and good. People were attracted. Here was no grim warning of God's judgement and perils ahead but a joyous promise of good and the blessings of God's created order. This was a new voice in the land bringing in a new day. People saw before them a new man such as they had not seen before, and no doubt some played with the thought that he might perhaps be the Messiah. But would he be in that simple peasant's garb, and with those strong work-worn hands? Yet there were the words, striking words, poetic words. Where did he obtain them? They were puzzled.

And then this great theme of his, the Kingdom of God which he was constantly touching on in metaphor, simile and parable, but never sharply defined, what was it? Apparently it was the rule of God in the hearts of men and women, it was doing God's will, it was making what God wanted sovereign over everything. This was how Jesus himself lived, it was the source of his power, 'not my will but thine be done', and this it was that he incorporated for his disciples and for us in the prayer which he taught: 'Our Father which art in heaven . . . , thy Kingdom come, thy will be done, on earth as it is in heaven.' So we have no excuse for not knowing. God's Kingdom is present when God's 'will is done on earth as it is in heaven'. And that Kingdom began to be at hand in a new way when Jesus was present because he himself lived God's will. This was the good news, this was the gospel. The Kingdom *had come*! Did hearers in Galilee understand? Do we understand? Can we grasp how living according to the will of God can be good news, can be a gospel, can make for salvation? Is not the western world living in the wake of the French Revolution, 'we want no authority please, not even of God, we only want liberty'. The teaching of Jesus was that true happiness only comes with doing the will of God, a gracious God, a God of justice and a God who cares for people.

2 THE WORKS OF JESUS

And now the actions of Jesus. Jesus did not only preach and teach, he worked for people. His words and his works, as I have already said, interlocked. If you turn to chapter 1 of St Mark's gospel you will read 'They came to Capernaum, and on the Sabbath he went to the synagogue and began to teach . . . Now there was a man in the

13

synagogue possessed by an unclean spirit . . . Jesus rebuked him: "Be silent", he said, "and come out of him". . . . "What is this? (said the onlookers). A new kind of teaching?"' It was of course. It was teaching interlocking with actions which speak louder than words. There are readers of the gospels who want to excise what are commonly called the miracles of Jesus. They want to leave us with Jesus' words but not his works. This however is to misread him entirely. Yes I know, some of the miracles are difficult to understand, let alone to believe, and some may have to be left in the 'pending' file, but to delete the wonderful works of Jesus wholesale is about as senseless as demanding an umbrella without the frame. The words and the works of Jesus interlock. The works are an integral part of the teaching. When he healed a blind man for whom no one cared he was saying aloud what kind of God he is that he was proclaiming. When he associated freely with the outcasts and sinners he was preaching as powerful a sermon on the love of God for us all that could ever be. And when he raised to life the only son of a widow who had made no request of him at all, he was crying aloud that God is ready to come to our aid before we even think of approaching him. What a God of Grace! What an inspiring Kingdom of God! How very much the opposite of repressive!

And now turn to the fourth gospel in the New Testament, St John's Gospel, the last to be written and different in many ways from the other three. But miracles are there, only they are called 'signs'. And this is what they were for those who had eyes to see, they were signs of the presence of the Kingdom of God in the world now come in the works of Jesus. The miracles (so called) were not therefore simply works of philanthropy, encouraging a concern for welfare on behalf of the needy whoever they may be, laudable as is that ministry. They are disclosure points of God's presence and of his attitude to mankind and gracious attitude. In a way the miracles are parables calling for interpretation, examples of which are found in St John's Gospel. Notable is the account of the feeding of the five thousand with five barley loaves and two small fish. It is recounted in all four gospels and must therefore be seen as of paramount importance. It constituted in fact a turning point in the ministry of Jesus for on the strength of it the crowds who witnessed it sought to make him their king and he was forced to escape them, earning as a result a new hostility for this refusal. John however saw further. He saw in this miraculous feeding a parable of how Jesus feeds with spiritual food those who turn to him. He is in fact the Bread of Life, a truth brought home to Christian congregations ever since in the Holy Communion: Christians are fed with the sacramental bread. This is a mystery not easy to explain and may occasion opposition. John, reading below the surface of the miracle of the feeding of the five thousand, brought out this interpretation and presented it as the teaching of Jesus, which undoubtedly it was, though not given as part of that historical event. What St John has provided in chapter 6 of his gospel is *event plus interpretation*, the wonderful work of feeding the five thousand and the presentation of Jesus as the Bread of Life.

3 THE KINGDOM OF GOD IN THE FUTURE

I have made the point that Jesus heralded the Kingdom of God as a present reality. Hear my text again from Mark 1.14, 15: 'Now after John was arrested, Jesus came into Galilee, preaching the gospel of God, and saying, "The time is fulfilled, and the kingdom of God is at hand; repent, and believe in the gospel."' And it is quite clear that he called for his disciples, and for us, to work to bring in that Kingdom as far as we are able by preaching and teaching the principles of that Kingdom as set forth in what is called 'the Sermon on the Mount' and in other parts of his teaching. But is the Kingdom of God only a *present* experience? Is it only partly and imperfectly realized in our world as we know it? Is there not to be fulfilment when the Kingdom of God will be manifested in power and glory? Some scholars have denied this. They will only allow what is called 'realized eschatology'. They admit that Jesus did speak of a future time when the Kingdom of God would come in its fullness at the end of history, indeed this cannot be denied from any straight reading of the gospels but they assent that this second coming, or coming again of Jesus, has been replaced in the fourth gospel by the coming of the Holy Spirit and we should so replace it. This however has not found favour and the promise of the second coming, and the Kingdom of God's dawning in the future (though *when* is unknown), has been held as belonging to the teaching of Jesus.

*   *   *

I come back now to where I began. If you wanted to describe what some historical person, such as Winston Churchill was really like you would have to tell both of what he said and what he did, and the words and the works interlock. So it is with the historical Jesus.

We must become acquainted with his teaching and with his actions. The gospels have made this possible. Be careful therefore to 'read, mark, learn and inwardly digest' them. You cannot be an informed Christian in default of this study. Only so is it possible to know the historical Jesus. Only so is it possible to know the God he lived and preached.

4

THE ATTRACTIVE JESUS

As long as they have the bridegroom with them, there can be no fasting.

MARK 2.19 (NEB)

Let me begin by drawing you an absurd picture. Actually it derives from St Mark's gospel, in fact from the text I have just quoted: 'As long as they have the bridegroom with them, there can be no fasting.' Here is a wedding party in progress. The bride and the bridegroom are, of course, the central figures, all dressed up in their best clothes as indeed are all the guests, and there are plenty of them, but everyone has a solemn face, not to say a downright glum face. There is no conviviality in the room whatsoever. And you look across to the side tables which are completely unbedecked with flowers, and there isn't a bottle of wine anywhere to behold, nor any glasses, nor a single plate of 'eatables'. You ask: has the van due to deliver these goods crashed on the way? Have the caterers muddled up the dates? And you are told 'No, nothing of the kind, the bridegroom wanted it like this, a wedding is a solemn affair, he wanted no hilarity whatever'. Looking around you have to comment 'Well, he has certainly succeeded, I've never seen a more miserable crowd of people in my life' . . . Of course this picture is absurd. It is impossible to *have* a party without freedom to talk, laugh and generally be light-hearted, stimulated by good things to eat and drink on the side tables. A wedding party and fasting simply *cannot* combine. The idea is absurd. Sadness is out, joyfulness is in.

1 NO SADNESS

So my text: 'As long as they have the bridegroom with them, *there can be no fasting.*' It is a practical impossibility. Now these are the words of Jesus and he was forced to utter them because some people were offended by the obvious cheerfulness, buoyancy and lack of

17

restraint on the part of his disciples gathered round him, and what was worse, he himself was obviously more than happy with it all. They couldn't square this light-heartedness with a serious religious leader. They looked to him to be solemn if not sad.

I have told this story before but I will repeat it because it is the best illustration I know of the text I am trying to expound and it took place in my presence. I was a curate then, and fairly new in a parish in the York diocese. The Archbishop, the famous William Temple, reckoned to possess one of the finest intellects in Europe, was the guest at a luncheon for clergy. I was seated at the lowest end of the table as far away as possible from the great man. But what surprised me was the uproarious laughter from his end of the table that punctuated the whole meal, and most noticeable of all was the Archbishop's laugh, so loud and infectious, making it impossible for anyone anywhere near him not to be drawn into his merriment. When the party was over and I had returned to the Rectory I commented on this to the Rector. I noticed how his face fell. 'Yes, I know', he said, 'a great many people reckon that buoyant laughter unbecoming in an Archbishop', and I could see he thought so himself. The general view was that a religious leader ought to be solemn.

Jesus wasn't a bit solemn. I know no text in the gospels which proves this more clearly than the one I have quoted from Mark 2.19 and copied in Matthew and Luke: 'As long as they have the bridegroom with them, *there can be* no fasting.' Apparently solemnity and sadness in Jesus' presence was an utter impossibility, they simply could not coexist—telling us plainly what he was like and why twelve young men, and many more than twelve, were fascinated by his lively company. They might not understand all he said, they might be puzzled about his identity but they adored him, no other word will do. They were prepared to leave their jobs in order to continue in his presence, they followed him 'up hill and down dale', caught by the spell of his personality, ever ready to stand apart from the religious authorities who were dead set against their hero.

2 HUMOUR

Lord Hailsham in his book *The Door Wherein I Went*, published by Collins in 1975 wrote about the historical Jesus:

As I reflected upon this, I came to the conclusion that the first thing we must learn about him is that we should have been absolutely entranced by his company. Jesus was irresistibly attractive as a man. The man whom they crucified was intensely fond of life, and intensely vital and vivacious. He did not wish to die. He was the last person to be associated with suffering. They called him a winebibber. They abused him for the company he kept. What was it, do you suppose, that kept Mary at his feet when Martha was scurrying about getting the dinner? Was it a portentous commentary on Holy Scripture? I feel sure that it was simply that she found his company actually enthralling.

Complaints are sometimes made that there are no jokes in the gospels. It is just as well that there are not; nothing dates so much as an old joke, nothing separates one race of people, one class of people, from another so much as what is thought to be funny. Recently there was a radio programme entitled *What Makes Different People Laugh?* The divergences were quite astonishing. Different nationalities have almost opposite ideas of what they consider humorous; in ignorance of this, deep offence can be caused. It is just as well therefore that there is no record in the gospels of Jesus telling jokes, much as Englishmen in particular might unthinkingly regret this. Yet did nothing funny never happen in Jesus' presence, leaving him all but overcome with laughter? What about that incident at the very beginning of his Galilean ministry (Luke 5.5 and 6). Two fishermen on the lake with long faces because they had fished the long night through and not a single fish was there to show for it. In and out they had hauled those heavy wet nets and all to no avail. And there was Jesus standing on the shore fresh in the morning light and calling 'Put out into deep water and let down your nets for a catch'. With an understandable grudge they did so and now there were so many slippery fish slapping about in the boat that they could scarcely stand. 'You wanted fish! You've got 'em.' Look at those fishermen's faces now. Jesus looked. Are you going to tell me he wasn't laughing?

Then that other day when four kind men lifted their friend up off the floor because, poor man, he couldn't walk, being a paralytic, and lowered him through a hole they made in the roof of the building where Jesus was. What a way to pay a visit to the doctor! Through the roof! This wasn't gate-crashing, it was roof-crashing! And Jesus looking up in the midst of his teaching session saw four brown faces looking down on him through the hole as they lowered their patient on his bedding. Are you going to tell me Jesus didn't laugh then? What a funny story for the next dinner party! Oh yes,

Jesus attended dinner parties, and he didn't sit there (recline there) dumb. He was the life and soul of the gathering.

There is more that could be told. What an unrelieved solemn business we make of that triumphal ride into Jerusalem on Palm Sunday as we have come to call it. But it was only a little donkey on which he was mounted. Never till then broken in. Did it kick? Did it buck? Or did it walk quietly like an old and well-tried beast? Which ever way, I suggest, the face of Jesus was wreathed in smiles. And the people by the roadside loved what they saw. They went wild with enthusiasm. Are you going to tell me Jesus sat on that little creature, his feet nearly touching the ground, with a poker face? If you do, I have to say, I do not think you have seen the real Jesus.

There are people who by their very presence are a benediction to the community. I was reading the other day an obituary notice of a well-respected former member of the House of Commons. What he was chiefly remembered for was the way he was able to turn any solemn debate into an occasion for a few well-timed outbursts of mirth, lifting the occasion out of the slough of depression on to a plane where an answer to the problem in hand became at least visible. Thank God for funny men, in a committee, in the army, in academic lecture rooms as well as in the pub. For our sanity and welfare I believe God, in his wisdom and mercy, has provided us with a limited number of comedians in life.

3 SENSITIVITY

Now I am not suggesting for one moment that the historical Jesus was a lightweight. He could come in an instant where people were because of his astonishing speed in perception, being, supersensitive to both men and women, registering in himself their feelings. He would rejoice with those who were rejoicing and weep with those who were weeping, quick to respond as the individual or group required. But the overall impression was of remarkable equipoise, a countenance where whatever clouds crossed it on account of what he saw and felt around him the sunshine would quickly break out. This is why people followed him in droves and hung upon his words. They longed to know the secret of his remarkable serenity whatever happened.

Of course the secret was that he lived close to God. His mission was to make God known, the God he himself knew intimately. He was not out to proclaim himself. After the resurrection when the gospels came to be written the evangelists proclaimed what his words and his works *signified* and, as it were, put words into his mouth, true words, but he did not, as he went about Galilee and Judaea, proclaim himself. He preached a God 'slow to anger and of great kindness' and when people met him, in person, watched him and heard him, they could believe his message, and it was a message of good tidings about God, a gospel.

Human nature, alas, is such that the very sight of poise, equanimity and serenity maddens a proportion of it. This is a fact which stares us in the face in the modern world. Beautiful buildings are hideously defaced by vandals, for no other reason than that they are beautiful; or out of resentment, by people who haven't a job, or are short of money and a house in which to live (conditions which need to be remedied and ought to be remedied). But not all adversities can be remedied. There are physical and mental deformities with which some have to live. It was not however the poor and the maimed who worked for the crucifixion of Jesus for they knew he cared for them, it was the secure and well-heeled in the places of privilege. They came to loathe the joy which Jesus' presence brought to people so they determined to stamp it out.

4 THE TELLTALE OF JESUS' PRESENCE

I come back to my text 'As long as they have the bridegroom with them there can be no fasting': Mark chapter 2, verse 19. I could have read on: 'But the time will come when the bridegroom will be taken away from them, and on that day they will fast.' I wonder if, as has been suggested, these words represented the *disciples' comment* on the awful blank they felt when Jesus was taken away and crucified. The thick blackness emphasized by contrast how radiant had been his presence while it was with them. It was as if the sun had been obliterated and there was no more joy, only fasting and sadness.

There is a little post-Resurrection story told by St Luke (24.28–32) which I think speaks volumes. Two disciples, bereft and miserable, walking to Emmaus outside Jerusalem. And they were joined by the risen Christ whom they did not recognize till—and this is the revealing part of the narrative—they all three at their journey's end sat down at a table and their guest took bread, said a blessing, broke it and gave it to them. They were suddenly taken back to the old times, those meals they attended, those happy times

21

of fellowship, table fellowship. What laughter! What freedom! What buoyant conversation! It was the memory of *this radiance* that caused them to know that they were in contact with the real Jesus; he was like that, always like that, there could be no possible doubt.

I am not sure that we Christians always reflect the radiance of the Master we profess to serve. Could it be said that churches are always happy places? Perhaps we need to see Jesus as he really was. Perhaps I, the preacher, need to see him again as he really was and to follow in his footsteps. I think to some limited extent the Church has caught something of the joy of her Lord or she could never have survived till this present day. But we need to keep the buoyancy of our Lord ever before us, not forgetting that he came to show us what the eternal God is like. So 'lift up your hearts! We lift them up unto the Lord.'

5

THE STRONG MAN

*No one can break into a strong man's house and make off with
his goods unless he has first tied the strong man up; then he can
ransack the house.*

MARK 3.27 (NEB)

This seems pretty obvious, scarcely worth the trouble of putting
into words. 'No one can break into a strong man's house . . . unless
he has first tied the strong man up.' But is it obvious that the strong
man here is Jesus of Nazareth? How many of us, how few of us,
think of him as a strong man. Are not our ideas of him still tinged
with Victorian religion's sentimentality—a meek, compassionate
creature, easily pushed around, the 'pale Galilean' as one writer
called him. Let me tear up this picture.

1 STRONGER THAN JOHN THE BAPTIST

St Mark tells a different story. He begins first of all depicting in
vivid colours John the Baptist his forerunner, the one who prepared
for him his public stage. John the Baptist, a man dressed in a coarse
coat of camel's hair with a leather belt around his waist. He lived
in the terrifying harsh desert wastes east of the Jordan river sup-
plementing his meagre diet with the little this barrenness provided
—locusts and wild honey. The last description of him imaginable
would be weakness. A man needed to be tough indeed even to sur-
vive there. And when people encountered him down at the river
conducting his ministry of baptism they were all at once reminded
of the mighty prophet Elijah, a giant if ever there was one in Israel's
history. This however is what we should notice. This supremely
strong man cried out to the crowds by the river 'After me comes
one who is mightier (who is stronger) than I'. And that one did
come. His name was Jesus of Nazareth. And before he ascended
the platform John the Baptist had prepared, he himself spent time
in that same wilderness where wild beasts roamed, testing and

strengthening his vocation. John the Baptist was a strong man and though Jesus was certainly not rugged like John, nor was he dressed in a coarse coat of camel's hair, he was exceedingly strong. Understandably, then, did he counter his opponents in Galilee with the words 'No one can break into a strong man's house . . . unless he has first tied the strong man up'. He was the strong man.

Now you could be thinking that I am representing Jesus as a strong man as a kind of reaction against sentimental pictures of him. This is not so. St Mark's story, without frills and literary decoration, opens with stories of Jesus' whirlwind thrusting activity as if there were not a moment to lose. And the crowds pressed upon him, pestering him for his attention but he never let up in his healing and preaching ministry, even meals had to be curtailed. His family noting this reckoned he had gone out of his mind and sought to restrain him. Who but a very strong man could withstand this pressurized activity? And who but a very strong man could address in the open air the crowds that gathered to hear him, one such said to number five thousand? And the emotional output involved in healing sick folk day after day, week after week! He said himself that power went out from him in the case of healing a woman suffering from a twelve-year-long haemorrhage. He drained his strength to meet people's need. And we read how his twelve disciples, strong young men, lagged behind him on the road to Jerusalem; they saw him striding ahead of them. Climbing the mountain of Transfiguration, possibly Hermon, presented no problem. And those penetrating eyes of his! A strong man indeed, but was he not compassionate with the weak and ailing? Was he not gentle? Did he not welcome little children to him and they were not in the least afraid? Yes, indeed, but what is more impressive than to see a strong man tender with the weak? This was Jesus, strong *and* gentle. With this double characteristic he towered above his forerunner John the Baptist.

The historical Jesus was not therefore a person of no great consequence in Galilee and Judaea. Never would the religious *and political* authorities have banded together as they did to plot his death were they not afraid of his commanding strength in the community. They set traps but the traps failed to ensnare him. They attempted to embroil him with the law but his repartee under attack left them standing on occasions even earning the satisfaction of the onlookers. And you say to me, Yes, but in the end they got him, they caught and crucified him. Yes, but he could have slipped their grasp as did his disciples. No, he deliberately gave himself up because sacrifice was the essential constituent of his ministry; in saying which, no doubt I have crossed over from history into

24

theological interpretation, but it is forced on me by what happened.

I reiterate what I have been at pains to stress; the historical Jesus was a strong man and maybe in the light of the crucifixion we can begin to catch a glimpse of the depth of meaning in his own words, 'No one can break into a strong man's house and make off with his goods unless he has first tied the strong man up; then he can ransack the house'. At the last Jesus let his opponents tie him up but—and this is the point to notice—they did not thereby ransack the house. The crucifixion, celebrated by Easter, has done more to furnish the Christian household than any other of his ministries. Jesus won by the tying up. He conquered by the cross.

2 THE SHAPE OF THE MINISTRY

Now a further reflection on the strength of Jesus. It made his ministry take the shape it did. Let me spell this out.

Jesus began his ministry as a preacher in the synagogues of Galilee, a popular preacher with a strong message of God's care for people, all people, reinforced by works of healing. Wherever he went crowds flocked to see him and hear him and if possible to touch him. There was in fact a revival of religion. It had been initiated by John the Baptist, shallow maybe, but more widespread than had been witnessed for many a long day. For Jesus there was however a special problem, a technical one—he was unauthorized. Therein lay the seeds of trouble to come. The official religious leaders whose ministries aroused no spontaneous enthusiasm were jealously opposed; they became dead set on putting an end to this uncertificated freelance Rabbi. But how? This was their difficulty. He was so strong. Strong in himself and in the popular regard. Perhaps not surprisingly, he soon found synagogues closed to him. So began his ministry in the open away from the towns. Then looking into the future he foresaw that even this public ministry would come to an end. He must therefore choose representatives to carry on his ministry and eventually extend it. So the twelve disciples came to be called. They would live with him, watch him, be taught by him and be sent out on a trial mission, all part of their training. This training of the twelve would occupy a large part of Jesus' work.

We can therefore distinguish three distinct groups which Jesus bore in mind in his preaching and teaching: the great crowds of enthusiastic but for the most part shallow followers: his intimate band of twelve disciples; and the hostile religious authorities listening carefully but critically bent on destroying him. How then was he to accommodate three such diverse groups in his preaching and teaching? The method he chose was to speak in parables. Parables had been employed by Jewish teachers before him but his parables became distinctive, so distinctive that parables have come to be associated with his name.

The first of his parables was addressed to the crowds that had flocked to hear him. Not all the parables were spoken in this kind of setting but this one was. It is the parable of the sower (see Matthew 13, Mark 4 or Luke 8). Perhaps a sower sowing his seed, carrying out his task, was actually visible to the listening crowds that day. In any case the scene was familiar enough. What surprises us would not surprise them – the sower scattering his seed by hand indiscriminately, some falling on the pathway, some in stony ground and some among the thorns. He was not selective about the soil into which it would fall. This was standard practice in Galilee. Not surprisingly, as we would judge, only a proportion of the seed sown came to fruition because only a proportion happened to fall into good soil. What is surprising is that according to Jesus, so it is with the word of God. It is broadcast liberally but only in a proportion of the hearers has it any lasting effect in their lives, indeed, only a proportion seem able to make sense of what they hear. We can imagine people in the crowds listening to Jesus turning blank faces and shaking their heads. What on earth is he talking about? We know how a sower sows his seed. But this was Jesus' comment as he watched his hearers. 'You do not understand this parable? How then are you to understand any parable?' So as one scholar has put it, 'The parables of Jesus were *teasers*'. They were meant to be. They raised questions leaving the hearers, if they have the will, to shape their own answers. On the surface they seem easy enough, no great acumen is required to understand what the sower is doing when he sows his seed. Like all the parables, the background is always the world we know, the everyday world, earthy, down to earth, anything but heavenly; all of which means that in Jesus' understanding the natural and the spiritual are not contrary to each other or, to put the matter rather more bluntly, we can learn of God from nature if we have the eyes to see.

I must add an important footnote here. Not all the parables by any means were addressed to the crowds or even to the disciples. Some were spoken at dinner parties in the course of general conversation, for Jesus on occasion accepted invitation to them. Some parables came into being as table talk, others as enigmatic replies in conflict situations. We shall touch on these in another sermon.

3 STRENGTH THROUGH BELIEVING

Come back to the text. Jesus was the strong man. What has this to say to us? It has this to say. The men and women who believe in him absorb into themselves by *believing* something of his strength, strength of character, strength of purpose, strength of compassion. Feebleness is never the consequence of faith in Jesus. Quite the reverse. It is even possible that spiritual strength can contribute to physical vigour. It acts like a seed, a tiny seed, but it grows when it falls into good ground as in the parable of the sower which Jesus told. What is important is that the picture of the historical Jesus be kept as clearly as is possible within our sight in Christian worship and discipleship. We must see Jesus as best we can and as much as we can if we are to believe in him. We cannot believe in someone of whom we know almost nothing. What can be more plain then that the duty of the Church, specially in its preaching, is to help people to see the historical Jesus, the strong man? This is the starting point for spiritual vigour and vitality. As Charles Wesley put it,

> Strong in the Lord of Hosts,
> And in his mighty power;
> Who in the strength of Jesus trusts
> Is more than conqueror.

6

THE MEN JESUS WANTED

*He then went up into the hill-country and called the men he
wanted; and they went and joined him. He appointed twelve as his
companions, whom he would send out to proclaim the Gospel, with
a commission to drive out devils. So he appointed the twelve: to
Simon he gave the name Peter; then came the sons of Zebedee,
James and his brother John, to whom he gave the name Boanerges,
Sons of Thunder; then Andrew and Philip and Bartholomew and
Matthew and Thomas and James the son of Alphaeus and
Thaddaeus and Simon, a member of the Zealot party, and Judas
Iscariot, the man who betrayed him.*

MARK 3.13–19

In this sermon I propose talking about the twelve disciples of Jesus
as they are commonly called; *when* he chose them and *why*; and a
little about them as a body. They were not impressive men indeed
at the tail end of the list there has always been some uncertainty
even about their actual names except for the notorious Judas
Iscariot. But at the head of the list Peter, James and John stand out,
and to some extent Andrew. We shall come to this later.

1 THE SELECTION

First we must understand how Jesus began his ministry without
them. He stepped up on the page of history alone. No one put him
forward, no organization was behind him, even his family hung back
from giving him support. He appeared as a lone prophet or preacher
dressed in the five articles of clothing everyone wore, neither rich
nor 'down and out'—a headdress, an outer cloak and an undergar-
ment, a girdle and sandals: nothing to mark him out. He spoke
Aramaic, a dialect of Hebrew, possibly with a Galilean accent and
maybe a smattering of Latin and Greek, for the Roman and Hellenic
civilizations had impressed their mark on the life of Galilee and

28

Judaea. He appeared as he essentially had been—a provincial carpenter. In no way could it be said that the impact he made consisted in externals but entirely in his own person. This was, and has always been, the mystery of Jesus. The trappings of greatness were simply not there.

He began a public ministry according to St John's gospel in Judaea and was impressive not only to all and sundry but also to a few upper-class people (the name of one such, Nicodemus, has come down to us). They did not however ally themselves with him, for he was not, as might be said today, 'out of the right drawer of society'. Yet he was as calmly and authoritative himself in their presence as in that of a Samaritan woman divorced five times (see John, chapter 4).

Then he moved on to Galilee and soon everyone was talking about him on account of his arresting preaching and the works of healing which accompanied his ministry. Jesus in fact became famous. Wherever he went he was surrounded by crowds. They never left him and he never left them, except to escape at times for private prayer, so utterly dedicated was he to his ministry. He gave himself to people, scarcely pausing to eat. Then there came the momentous day when he went up into the hill country in Galilee, the crowds trailing after him. In a loose kind of way they were all his disciples for they followed him hanging upon his words. But the time had come for him to prepare for the future and abandon his solo ministry. He needed a band of close companions about him. He himself selected whom they were to be, twelve men whom he had watched carefully and clearly knew. Peter, James, John and Andrew headed the list. He had encountered them in a dramatic way in their boat on the lake.

2 THE MEN THEMSELVES

We look at these twelve men. First why twelve? Why not six or ten? We are not told but it is hard not to see in the choice a deliberate linking to the twelve tribes of Israel with the veiled hint that he, Jesus was the Messianic King foretold by the prophets. Was this dangerous? Might it not put political ideas of greatness to come, in the minds of these simple men, in some restored Kingdom of Israel? Possibly. But Jesus ran the risk. He would teach these men and anyway events would change their perspectives. In any case we notice that he himself chose these men. They did not offer to be his companions in his ministry and they were not elected by the main body of followers. There was no democracy. Furthermore all twelve chosen were men. No doubt there are people today who regret this, there should have been some women, perhaps six men and six women. Some think there would have been had the selection been made at some other time than the first century with its patriarchal culture. Who knows? The only hard fact is Jesus *appointed* (Mark 3.14 RV, the Greek word here is *made*) twelve men, all Galileans except Judas Iscariot, who is thought to have come from Kerioth beyond the Jordan river and was therefore Judaean and, in that sense, an outsider among the twelve.

With the possible exception of Matthew, who was quick at figures, a kind of 'smart Alec', they were poor provincials with little facility in reading and writing and of no social standing whatsoever. Their choice does not however represent a bias to the poor and uneducated on the part of Jesus. No other selection was open to him, for the privileged classes of his day, including the religious, affected to despise him. They certainly did not believe in him or commit themselves in any way to him. He was outside their reckoning. Even so the sheer simplicity of these twelve men gave them one advantage, they were supremely qualified to act as witnesses to the works and words of Jesus. They lacked the capacity to philosophize or theologize but they could say what they had seen and heard, and came to find themselves in a unique position to do so for they actually lived with him and moved about with him as did no one else. This is the basis of the importance of the twelve disciples. We ought also to notice that they were chosen not only to be his companions but in order that he might send them out to proclaim the gospel and to engage in a ministry of exorcism. That time had not yet come, nor were they ready for it. They needed to be taught, and what hard work they made of it! The gospels are very honest in revealing their initial dim-wittedness. At times their slowness to understand all but exasperated Jesus, their teacher, but they stuck by him if not without a struggle (see John 6.67–71).

Of the twelve men Simon, to whom Jesus gave the name Peter (meaning a rock), was the most articulate though not invariably with forethought. Neither was he always rock-like. He had a terrible lapse at Jesus' trial, but he had a great future before and after he came to Rome and if he really did write the letter called 'First Peter' in the New Testament he must have progressed remarkably in learning, for its Greek is some of the most literary in the whole book, or maybe the wording, if not the content, was written by some competent helper. James and John were thoroughly loyal but inclined to hot-headedness. It is interesting that Jesus wanted such men near him. They were brothers, sons of Zebedee, whose wife Salome, their mother, was the sister of Mary, Jesus' mother. Andrew was Peter's brother. It is not difficult to see how well Jesus knew these four disciples. Philip was an earnest enquirer but slow. Bartholomew was known for his uprightness of character; Thomas was loyal but melancholy; Matthew (Levi) had been a tax collector and therefore a hated collaborator with the ruling authority but was called all on his own to follow Jesus. Little is known of James the son of Alphaeus. Who Thaddeus was is a puzzle, for he has three different names in the gospels; Simon, the eleventh man, had been a member of the Zealot Party, a revolutionary sect; a man with a strong political bias; apparently Jesus wanted him. Judas Iscariot 'became', as Luke puts it, the traitor. What a company of unlikes they were! It is to be wondered how they got along together, Matthew the ex-collaborator for instance with Simon the Zealot, or is it that the call by Jesus and his continual presence made it possible? They began to develop new priorities thereafter which blunted old hostilities. Perhaps this is one of the lessons to be learned from these twelve men.

3 A WORD OF GOD TO US

And now since this is not a lecture but a sermon we ought to enquire what word from God this aspect of the historical Jesus which we have been considering has to say to us.

First, surely, that God does not call only men and women with the capacity for leadership to be his servants and to engage in work for him. Only four of the twelve disciples stand out as possessing this gift, and three of the rest were insignificant as far as accomplishments were concerned and, maybe as persons. The Church does not only require leaders, too many would bring trouble. It is just as well therefore that we cannot all be leaders. But the converse is also true, there have to be leaders. An army without leaders is unthinkable, it could not operate and the same is true of any community, any group. The question is never 'do we need leaders?' but 'what kind of leaders do we need?'

The second observation from the call of the twelve disciples follows. If the simple type of men and women in the community, the less skilled and even the unskilled and the poorly educated are

31

not to be discounted as unsuitable for the service of God; neither are the elite, the intellectuals and the successful in business. The indispensable qualifications are faith and sincerity. What is more, there are areas of life where what might be called 'top grade' people would be a failure. Pity the academic who was sent to work as a priest in a slum, pity the people in a slum parish who had an academic as their pastor. There have been exceptions, glorious exceptions but exceptions they are. A variety of types are needed in the Christian ministry.

Thirdly we must recognize the differences among people, accept them for what they are and, to use a rough phrase, get along with them, not 'looking down on any'. People who live in the countryside are more aware of this than are the dwellers in the towns and big cities. Where would they be without the men who can cut hedges and clean out ditches? All men and women, whoever they are, whatever their occupation, should be respected.

But what about the rich man? Is he to be left out of God's family simply because of his riches? None of the twelve whom Jesus chose were conspicuous for possessions though Peter presumably owned a house by the lakeside in Capernaum and made it available for Jesus. And Matthew, at one time a tax gatherer, knew a great deal about money and no doubt once possessed a house far finer than Peter's. And then there were the well-to-do women who from their own resources supplied the needs of the men whom Jesus called. And Joseph of Arimathea, who provided Jesus' burial place at the end, was sufficiently wealthy to possess a tomb ready for himself in a select garden close to Jerusalem's centre. Riches do not automatically debar from the fellowship of God's people; only if riches are counted as a kind of God, only if they are reckoned as the be-all and end-all of the good life.

Come back to the hill country in Galilee that day when Jesus went up to it and, out of the crowds who followed him there, selected twelve men. If we have imagination we can see the look of surprise on the faces of each one of them. What me? Surely not me? What qualifications have I to be chosen to be the companion of this Jesus and to be sent out as his representative? None of us should ever lose a sense of wonder that we are privileged to possess the gift of faith and be a disciple of Christ because it is a gift; it is a privilege. We cannot make it come but when we have it our future may be surprising. The twelve disciples became the twelve apostles, pillars of the Christian Church. Were they not chosen for this?

7

JESUS THE TEACHER

When he saw the crowds he went up the hill. There he took his seat, and when his disciples had gathered round him he began to address them. And this is the teaching he gave.

MATTHEW 5.1–2 (NEB)

To visualize this scene is not difficult. This is one of the stories in the gospels people in general do not boggle at. There is no miracle here, nothing we cannot sit comfortably with and accept. Jesus, ascending a hill overlooking the Lake of Galilee and in drawing away from the crowds attracting their attention by doing so. Where was he going? What was he about to do? They trooped up behind him and watched him deliberately sit down and gather his recently appointed twelve disciples around him. Clearly this was to be a teaching session, not for the crowds apparently but they could overhear – at least, those at the front could overhear.

This was the setting for what has come to be called 'The Sermon on the Mount' though it was scarcely a sermon as we understand a sermon. The three chapters, 5, 6 and 7 in St Matthew's gospel, are far more likely to represent a summary of what Jesus said on this occasion and also what he said on a number of other occasions collected together to make a connected and structured whole. This is suggested by the fact that some of the teaching here is set down in St Luke's Gospel (6.20–49) as belonging to another occasion and to another place. Even so, these three chapters of St Matthew's gospel are important as telling us what it was that Jesus taught. Let me quote the text again: 'When he saw the crowds he went up the hill. There he took his seat, and when his disciples had gathered round him he began to address them. And this is the teaching he gave.'

1 THE KINGDOM OF HEAVEN

I wish we could see the faces of these twelve disciples as they listened to this teaching, and some of the crowds too who could

33

overhear. They must have registered utter astonishment, if not bewilderment, passing enquiring looks and pulled faces at each other. What is he saying? Have we really heard correctly? 'Fortunate are you poor people.' They did not feel fortunate at all. It was the rich who were fortunate, the well-heeled and the well-fed. And what was this which followed: 'for the kingdom of Heaven belongs to you'. The kingdom of heaven? But they wanted a kingdom on earth, most people do, with 'goodies' thrown in, and no oppressive overlords and no armed conflicts. The twelve disciples listened intently like new pupils in a class though understanding little of what was said, but they did gather that the kingdom of which Jesus spoke was something in the hearts of the people. It was not of this world, not something to be seen in space at all, neither here nor there; it was *a spiritual disposition*.

When the session broke up, not only the twelve disciples, for whom it was of special significance marking the beginning of their training by Jesus, but others also in the listening crowds must have remarked on the strangeness to their ears of all that they heard. 'This is all so new, we have never heard anything like this before. He said nothing for instance about us as the chosen people of God; nothing about the Jerusalem Temple as the guarantee of our national security; nothing about circumcision as essential for membership in God's kingdom. Is this Jesus a revolutionary then? Is he out to turn all our customs and traditions upside down? But he does not appear as a revolutionary, not at least as we have understood them. He actually said "Do not suppose that I have come to abolish the Law and the prophets. I did not come to abolish but to complete." And he even went on to add "I tell you this: so long as heaven and earth endure, not a letter, not a stroke will disappear from the Law until all that must happen has happened. If any man therefore sets aside even the least of the Law's demands, and teaches others to do the same he will have the lowest place in the Kingdom of Heaven, whereas anyone who keeps the Law and teaches others so will stand high in the Kingdom of Heaven."' But the little group of people walking away from this teaching session on the hill must have grown really excited when they recounted how Jesus had cut down to size the official ministers of religion who set themselves above everyone else on a supposed pinnacle of goodness and expected the whole community to recognize this. Emphatically he said 'I tell you, unless you show yourselves far better men than the Pharisees and doctors of the law, you can never enter the Kingdom of Heaven'.

And then they tried to remember some of the startling opening sentences:

34

How blest are those who know that they are poor; the Kingdom of Heaven is theirs. How blest are the sorrowful; they shall find consolation. How blest are those of a gentle spirit; they shall have the earth for their possession. How blest are those who hunger and thirst to see right prevail; they shall be satisfied. Now blest are those who show mercy; mercy shall be shown to them. How blest are those whose hearts are pure; they shall see God. How blest are the peacemakers; God shall call them his sons. How blest are those who have suffered persecution for the cause of right; the Kingdom of Heaven is theirs.

Nothing aggressive here. No trace of self-assertion, no hint of retaliation for wrongs suffered. Was this a blueprint of the kingdom of heaven? But where could it ever be realized? Then maybe one of those twelve disciples thinking hard wondered if perhaps it was already being realized before their very eyes in the person of Jesus himself who consistently puzzled them. He was of this world and then seemed to be not of this world, certainly not of its spirit. They continued their journey down the hill, the Sermon on the Mount, so called, was over. The first teaching session was ended. They kept thinking about it.

2 THE TEACHER AND THE TEACHING

Now we have to ask why it was that Jesus' hearers found his teaching arresting. First because the teacher was an arresting person. The teacher and the teaching can never be separated. This is true of any and every teacher. What the teacher is the teaching is. There can never be strong teaching if the teacher is a weak personality, never arresting teaching if the teacher is dull. The people of Galilee recognized in Jesus a man strong in himself and decisive in action before they sat down to hear what he had to say. When they heard what he had to say and how he said it they instinctively addressed him as Teacher, and this became in Galilee his customary title. That it was instinctive and not studied is obvious from the occasion when the disciples were in peril of their lives in a boat with Jesus asleep during a violent storm and they cried out 'Teacher, don't you care that we perish?' There was no time to formulate a polite address. Teacher, we can be certain, is how they saw Jesus. All manner of titles would, with the passage of time, come to be given him but at the outset of his ministry they consistently called him Teacher.

A second reason why his hearers found his teaching arresting was because of its novelty. It broke clean away from all that was commonly taught and practised in religious circles. I have already indicated that I think the so-called Sermon on the Mount in St Matthew's Gospel chapters 5 to 7 is probably a summary of what he said on this occassion and on a number of other occasions. Be that as it may, we can learn from it how fresh and how new was his teaching. Six times over in chapter 5 he repeated 'You have learned that our forefathers were told . . . *but what I tell you is* . . .'. Did no one mutter 'Who does he think he is?' They must have done. Clearly Jesus set himself up as the authority for the morality he advocated. There was to be no mechanical following of rules of conduct but a spontaneous attitude to right and wrong springing from the heart; and no ostentation in religious practices such as prayer, fasting and giving to charities. The religion he taught was humble and retiring and based on a belief in God as a gracious Father who wants his children to be contented, free from anxiety and cheerful. Certainly not judgemental of others, but instead leaving the judgement to God.

3 THE TEACHING MINISTRY

Now I can imagine some, especially those keen to promote evangelism commenting, Yes, all this about Jesus as a teacher is interesting but is it the heart of the gospel? Is not the gospel Christ crucified and risen, calling for our repentance and the living of a new life in the power of the divine Spirit? The answer is 'Yes'. And I have to agree that to accept Jesus chiefly as an inspired teacher, different *only in degree* from other of the world's great and inspiring teachers, is not the presentation which the New Testament offers. The story which the gospels have to tell builds up to the cross and resurrection as the climax and fulfilment of the ministry of Jesus. It does not run down to Good Friday and Easter as the anticlimax to a remarkable teaching ministry, which indeed it was. Even so, the teaching ministry is not to be overshadowed. It is the beginning of the Gospel. St Mark has made this plain in the opening words of his gospel, 'Here begins the Gospel of Jesus Christ', and the other three gospels follow his plan. The teaching of Jesus is given extensive coverage. We need to know what he said as well as what he did. Only so shall we encounter the historical Jesus.

In the Church today there is a widespread decline of a teaching ministry. This is a great loss. It is not enough that the Church should operate as a Eucharistic fellowship, not enough that it should support the weak, tend the sick and care about the underprivileged right and proper as are all these activities, but it must also *teach the faith* which undergirds and gives them their distinctive flavour. This means, among other activities, sermons on the historical Jesus, carefully and imaginatively prepared, and delivered in an arresting manner. For the Church to do this would be to follow in the steps of her Master who was an impressive and authoritative teacher. People called him 'Teacher'. They couldn't help it. This is what he obviously was.

8

A FAITH SUFFICIENT FOR STORMS

'Who is this, that even the wind and sea obey him?'
MARK 4.41 (RSV)

Not long after I had been appointed vicar of my first parish I was
asked to take on the extra duty of ministering to the patients of the
local Marie Curie Cancer Hospital for women. I embarked on it
with some fear and trembling, but I soon discovered that the fear
and trembling was a regular part of the patients' experience, though
bravely concealed. Once a week I used to conduct a short service
in the main ward; we struggled with a hymn and I gave a short
address. Time and time again my subject was the story of the storm
on the lake from St Mark's gospel able to be repeated at intervals
because the inmates of the ward changed, often, I am sorry to say,
through death. But the story never failed to grip the attention and
when after seven years I left for another parish one patient, a bit
of an artist, presented me with a large drawing she had secretly
made of Jesus standing up in the boat during the storm and calling
to the wind and waves 'Peace! Be still!' I kept that drawing.

Now it soon became clear to me that the verse in the narrative
which came home to them was 'Why are you afraid? Have you no
faith?' It spoke to their condition. I am going to preach on this story
but not on this text but the one which follows it. 'And they were
filled with awe, and said to one another, "Who is this, that even
the wind and sea obey him?"', and for this reason, that we might
catch a glimpse of the impression the historical Jesus made on the
people who encountered him in their day. So let me tell the story.

1 CROWDS OF PEOPLE

First notice the crowds of people. People were everywhere. They
had come from everywhere. They had crossed frontiers. They had
left homes. They had hobbled, groped and clutched at arms offered
for their assistance. There were blind people and deaf and diseased.

38

Some had to be carried or half carried. Stifling groans and sighs they shuffled along and could not or would not be hindered. They must reach this man from Nazareth who could heal people, so they heard, with a touch of hand or a word from his mouth. Everyone was talking about healing in a country where there was very little healing and no hospitals, no asylum and no infirmaries to speak of. The sick and broken were distressingly obvious in every community. They were encountered by the roadside and in all public places stretching out pathetic hands for help. And now there was this Jesus who healed people down by the Lake of Galilee; all sorts of people. No wonder there were crowds pushing and shoving, their numbers doubled, trebled, perhaps quadrupled by the inevitable sightseers. Now he wished to speak to them, and they wished to hear him speaking. Had they not been told of the astonishing reaction in the Capernaum synagogue when he mounted the pulpit? They wouldn't leave the lakeside where he was. But how could he address them pressing up close against him? So his disciples made their boat available—was it perhaps Peter's boat?—and with Jesus sitting in it pushed out a little from the shore, the crowds lining the beach. The water was as still as a duck pond, it usually was. On and on he went, teaching, illustrating and exhorting, he told parables like the famous one of the sower sowing his seed, till he was worn out. Public speaking is a strength-draining experience and Jesus was almost 'all in' by the evening. He must get away. 'Let us go to the other side of the lake', he said. It was quieter there, far fewer people, so the disciples pushed the boat out into the lake and Jesus made straight for the helmsman's seat at the rear, laid his head on the cushion and fell fast asleep—exhausted.

2 THE MAN IN THE BOAT

And now my question. How did those twelve men in the boat, those twelve disciples, see him? Time and time as the craft made its slow progress across the still water they must have contemplated his heavily sleeping figure on the cushion. A man of commanding authority certainly. Had they not themselves downed tools forthwith when he called them to follow him, some of them in that very boat? Men do not easily run that risk, but there was something about him. All manner of people were impressed in his presence. Even mentally deranged people, said in the thought-form of the time to be 'demon-possessed', sensed something and reacted. He

39

was, of course, a man. Was he not now fast asleep in the boat like any ordinary mortal? Yet he wasn't ordinary. Those astonishing healings of the sick witnessed by crowds. And that compelling speech of his. You had to listen. And his eyes. And his presence. But there are in the world individuals possessed of extraordinary gifts. They become the leaders in their community. Is this how the disciples saw Jesus, a quite extraordinary man, but a man all the same? They were puzzled.

Then suddenly their attention was diverted. The placidity of the lake was changing rapidly. Already waves were disturbing it deeply. Clearly one of the freak storms occasioned by the peculiar geographical situation of the lake, the proximity of mountains and the onrush of cold winds into the heat of the plain was about to break over them. The disciples in the boat were alarmed. In no time mounting waves broke into the boat and no amount of baling availed. Then they caught sight of Jesus still sound asleep like a trusting child. It angered them. They needed every scrap of assistance to keep afloat. Not surprisingly they rounded on him, shouting above the roar of the wind, 'Master, we are sinking! Do you not care?' (Mark 4.38 NEB). What now had become of their admiration for this man whose compassion for all who were in any kind of need had impressed not only them but the crowds swarming so recently about his person? Don't you care that we perish? Are you after all a non-caring leader?

Then the sleeper awoke, or stood up if that is what the Greek word used here means. He rebuked the wind and said to the sea, 'Hush! Be still!' The wind dropped and there was a dead calm (NEB). Did it? But if it did, why? Was it perhaps because the boat had been swept around a headland out of the wind into a patch of slack water? This is one modern view. Or has a natural occurrence been blown up into a miracle story, possibly on the basis of Psalm 89, verse 9: 'Thou rulest the raging of the sea: thou stillest the waves thereof when they arise'? After all, no man is able to order winds and waves about! No, but was the man in the boat who addressed the elements a man? He certainly looked every inch a man and was exhausted like a man. This is the problem of the historical Jesus which this story disturbingly sharpens.

Now we watch him. Did he seek to calm these frightened men? Did he speak kindly to them battered as they were by the storm? He did not. He uttered a stern rebuke: 'Why are you such cowards? Have you no faith even now?' Ought they to have known that it was contrary to reason, let alone faith, to think that the boat could go down to a watery grave with God incarnate in it? But had these

40

men at this stage any idea of Jesus as God incarnate? Yet ought they not to have trusted him after all they had seen him do for people?

As the boat ploughed its way across the lake now calm once more there must have been an awkward silence in the boat. They did not know what to say except to raise again the burning question 'Who then is this, that even the wind and the sea obey him?' Who indeed? The question has not gone away least of all in our modern world.

3 FEAR AND FAITH

And now the sharp rebuke of Jesus, 'Why are you afraid? Have you no faith?' Could it be addressed to us? We know what fear is, especially fear of the future in a fast changing world where the familiar landmarks are disappearing. Will even marriage go out of fashion? And what about my own position in the business world? Shall I be made redundant? And suppose I fall ill how shall we manage to keep our home going? And what about our children, what lies in store for them? Perhaps we need to ask if we believe that God is in our world, that God is in our own boat whatever storms seem to point to the contrary, even that he does not care about us. 'Master, don't you care that we perish?' With him we shall weather the storm even though we ship much water. Perhaps we need a rebuke for not believing. We have seen much and experienced much and been taught much that ought to have kindled the lamp of faith in our hearts. After all before us we have not only the historical Jesus but the Christ of faith, the risen Christ. We have more than those twelve disciples had at the stage in which this story of the storm on the lake depicts them. We ought to believe in the presence of God with us. We ought not to fear, we ought to exhibit courage. Faith and fear are opposites. It is the men and women of faith who achieve in their lives, come what may. And faith begins when we make up our mind about who Jesus is – 'Who then is this, that even the wind and sea obey him?' And faith has much to do with how we face up to the storms of life that from time to time blow across us all in this sometimes rough world.

41

9

THE LOCAL CARPENTER

Where did this man get all this?

MARK 6.2 (RSV)

Whenever I see in the newspaper, or hear on the radio, a mention of Sheringham on the north Norfolk coast, I sit up. The mention may be due to no more than that a small stretch of cliff has fallen, or a number of seals have been washed up on the shore, but I still sit up. Sheringham has no connexion with me now since my family moved away with me as a very small boy, and I have scarcely ever been back to it. But still I sit up when I hear it mentioned. Why? Because I was born there. Places of origin make a mark on us whether we are aware of the fact or not, they give us identity, even humanity which we should not feel if we were placeless persons. And everyone listening to me could substitute another place name for Sheringham and the story would fit.

1 NAZARETH

Jesus was connected with a place. He was consistently known as Jesus of Nazareth. He belonged there. He was brought up there. The people of Nazareth do not appear to have known that he was born in Bethlehem. He was a Nazarene and as such he died. The title over his cross read '*Jesus of Nazareth* King of the Jews' (John 19.19).

What sort of place was it? Certainly not a village nor a hamlet but a town, hardly a city, small of course, but all towns were small in those days. It was completely lacking in architectural distinction; the Jews, unlike the Greeks, did not possess this skill. For the most part their towns were a muddled collection of small houses, mostly single-roomed, threaded through with narrow winding streets which we might describe as alleys. The towns had no centre; no centre for meetings apart from a small space in front of the town gate.

Nazareth was built on the slope of a hill from the top of which a splendid panoramic view of all Galilee could be obtained. Lying off the main trade routes which nevertheless passed close by, it was not cut off from the news and gossip of the great world outside crisscrossed as it was by three cultures, Roman, Greek and of course Jewish. In Jesus' time only four miles north of Nazareth the great Greek city of Sepphoris was under construction. Essentially however Nazareth was a rural town, its simple economy based on the surrounding agricultural land where everyone lent a hand at harvest time. The suggestion is sometimes made that it was a notoriously evil place because of Nathaniel's remark quoted in John 1.46, 'Can any good thing come out of Nazareth?' Much more likely is the implication that if anyone were looking for learning or culture Nazareth would not be the place to go.

This then is where Jesus was brought up, attending the local synagogue and the local school. He had no training beyond what these provided and as soon as he was old enough he began work as a carpenter labouring with his hands (if this is what the Greek word *tektōn* means, though it could refer to a craftsman in wood, stone or metal). So he continued for some eighteen years, that is until he was about thirty (Luke 3.23), when he began to be known in the towns and villages of Galilee as a powerful preacher and healer earning such fame that it provoked an ugly jealousy on the part of the official religious leaders of the community. He therefore left Nazareth with his family, that is his mother and four brothers, to go and live in Capernaum down by the lake, his sisters remaining behind possibly because they had married and settled in Nazareth.

There came a Sabbath however when he revisited his old home town. He came as a preacher and healer with a reputation, and not alone but accompanied by his disciples. It was an occasion of importance for Nazareth. The synagogue was packed everyone agog to see and hear this local man of whom everyone was talking. And if we follow St Luke's account (4. 14–30) we can see him standing up to read and being handed the scroll of the prophet Isaiah by the chazzan or synagogue attendant. He found the place where it was written, and read out loud

The Spirit of the Lord is upon me, because he has anointed me to preach good news to the poor. He has sent me to proclaim release to the captives and recovering of sight to the blind, to set at liberty those who are oppressed to proclaim the acceptable year of the Lord.

43

He rewound the scroll and those who knew their scriptures waited, they waited for the words which follow, 'and the day of vengeance of our God'; but they waited in vain, the words never came. Clearly Jesus was not preaching God's vengeance, not even in Nazareth. Then he sat down, the accepted form for preaching. The eyes of everyone in the synagogue were fixed on him, surely not omitting his hands, large, strong, workman's hands. He began 'Today this scripture has been fulfilled in your hearing'.

2 JESUS THE ENIGMA OF NAZARETH

What followed astonished them—gracious diction; rhythmic sentences; phrases that lodged in the mind even at first hearing; picture language; but pointed and teasing; evoking a reaction on the part of the hearer. Not to pay attention to this preaching was impossible, it took hold of the whole congregation. They had never heard anything like it. But because the place was Nazareth it raised a question, overtaking the content of the sermon. 'Where did this man get all this? What is the wisdom given to him? What mighty works are wrought by his hands. Is not this the carpenter, the son of Mary and brother of James and John and Judas and Simon, and are not his sisters here with us?' So reads Mark 6, verses 2 and 3. 'And they took offence at him.'

Jesus was a puzzle to Nazareth for it reckoned it knew all there was to know about him. For years it was constantly encountering him in the alleyways. In the synagogue that Sabbath day however they realized that they did not in fact know him, he was an enigma. So, too, to his family and in a measure even to his disciples. He was close to them and yet he was apart from them. They were puzzled. People do not like being puzzled, especially by their neighbours. More than that the people of Nazareth felt insulted by Jesus. He had carried out his wonderful works, and they were wonderful, but why in Capernaum and the surrounding villages; why not in Nazareth his home town? And so he sensed a wall of opposition building up against him drawing forth this revealing comment, 'A prophet is not without honour, except in his own country, and among his own kin, and in his own house'. So the return visit to Nazareth was a failure (if we follow St Mark's account in chapter 6, 1 to 6)—not a total failure, a few responded and experienced for themselves the healing power of those hands of his when he laid them on sick people, but not many. Jesus was 'taken aback by their want of faith' (Mark 6.6 NEB). These were early days. He would meet it again.

But what did he say in the sermon? Obviously he did not end with his opening sentence 'The Spirit of the Lord is upon me', though that was arresting enough, being tantamount to an explanation why he, an ex-carpenter, was now a preacher. And what was this about the Spirit of the Lord? They knew nothing about this anointing with the Spirit in the Jordan river before he undertook any public ministry at all. No one knew, not even John the Baptist who baptized him. Only to him was the disclosure made that he was God's 'beloved Son', only he knew that he was called to a special ministry and that his life was wide open to the power of God as he submitted to his will, but he was conscious of it that Sabbath day when he occupied the seat of the preacher in the Nazareth synagogue. 'The Spirit of the Lord is upon me.'

But he offended Nazareth with his sermon. He offended because he told of the breadth of God's care for people. Blatantly he cut clean across the narrowness of the Nazarenes' conception as to who should benefit. Jewish race, not need, in their view was the determining factor. Jesus cut across this by reminding them of how in time of famine Elijah, the great prophet, was sent only to the relief of a widow woman in *Sidon*, Gentile territory, what lower grade could there be? And how Naaman, a Syrian, a foreigner, was the only leper cleansed by Elisha, the prophet, when there were lepers in plenty in *Israel*. The congregation rose up in arms at what they saw as an attack on their own privileged racial position. The Jews were God's chosen people and no one else. Is this an overstatement 'they rose up in arms'? But St Luke 4.28–30 reads 'When they heard this all in the synagogue were filled with wrath. And they rose up and put him out of the city, and led him to the brow of the hill on which their city was built, that they might throw him down headlong. But passing through the midst of them he went away.' Were his captors overawed by his person when he was in their grasp? Does this point to the strength of the impression Jesus made on people? Or was this some kind of miracle of Providence determining that he should not be killed outside Nazareth at the start of his ministry but outside Jerusalem at the close? I have to confess I do not know, but I wonder ...

3 THE DANGER OF FAMILIARITY

What does all this say to us? Surely the message concerns the danger of familiarity in religion. We know it all or we think we know it all and are deeply offended if someone should suggest otherwise. Then our name is Nazareth. We know the Book of Common Prayer backwards. We have always been 'up front' with the Alternative Service Book. We use the latest translation of the Bible. We have taken a course of advanced theological studies. We know all about source criticism, form criticism, redaction criticism; and as for organized religion we could almost write the agenda of the General Synod. Because of all this we reckon we know all about the historical Jesus, but do we? Does he really make any impression on us? Or is his name little more than a formula it is customary to repeat? I tell you, no, this story of the visit to Nazareth tells us, there is a grave danger in religious familiarity, it can bring us to the point where our religion has nothing to say to us or at least nothing that we can *hear*. There is, I regret to remind you, such a thing as *dead orthodoxy*, and it can be evangelical, catholic or liberal, and if perhaps you don't quite know what I mean, then maybe you are in a better position to see and hear Jesus than those who reckon they know it all.

I want to stress this point about the enigmatic character of the historical Jesus. Perhaps 'mystery' would be a more apt word than 'enigma'. We can never really know him. No one ever really knew him. This was the foolishness of Nazareth that it thought it did. 'Is not this the carpenter, the son of Mary, the brother of James and Joseph and Judas and Simon? Are not his sisters with us?' (Mark 6.3). There are those today, or perhaps I ought to say in this century, who speak of *Jesus before Christ* and are confident that they have found the real figure because shorn of all the subsequent accretion summed up in the title 'Christ', they have cut the Church's Christ down to size, a person whom they nevertheless count as admirable on account of what he said, not least in his Sermon on the Mount (so called), but on this reckoning there is no distinctive mystery about him beyond what is mysterious in any and every outstanding man or woman. There is no one to worship.

I have to tell you there is no escape from the necessity of faith in Jesus of Nazareth. I do not mean credulity or the total rejection of reason, but the time will come when we shall have to venture into the partially unknown and say 'All right, I will believe in this man'. The extent of our decision to believe may be elementary, it may be profound, but unless we are willing to make it, our religion will do very little for us even as Jesus was able to do very little for the people of Nazareth. Familiarity and unbelief could be the label fixed up over this town. Poor Nazareth, how Jesus must have sighed as he saw the blind, the sick and the lame for whom he could do nothing. They thought they knew all about him because they knew his background, they wouldn't *believe*, that was the tragedy of the Nazarenes.

10

HEALING BY CONTACT

'If I touch even his clothes, I shall be cured.'
MARK 5.28 (NEB)

A short time ago my eye was caught by an advertisement in the newspaper for a new and successful treatment for arthritis. I have forgotten what it was, so don't ask me afterwards! But so common is the ailment and so painful and limiting that I can imagine crowds of people writing to the newspaper for information. How wonderful to be free of those aching limbs! How wonderful to be able to negotiate the staircase again! I understand. I have seen what arthritis can do.

1 TOUCHING

Today I bring to your attention the case of a woman, not old, perhaps only in her late twenties, for whom life through a physical ailment was scarcely a life at all, certainly not as a woman interpreted it. She couldn't marry, she couldn't have children, she couldn't engage in any work where contact with other people was normal. She was alone in her world, banished and avoided, and all through no fault of her own. She suffered from an uterine haemorrhage which according to the hygienic rules of the community to which she belonged rendered her unclean. Her misery had dragged on for twelve long years and she saw no end to it. It wasn't so much the pain that troubled her as the ostracism it caused and the consequent loneliness. Loneliness can be a slow killer and she felt she was being killed. Not that she hadn't tried to find a cure. All her savings had gone on doctors but to no avail. She was even worse. All they could offer were quack remedies, like sitting at the cross roads with a cup of wine in her hand and someone deputed to creep up behind and shout three times 'Be healed of thy issue of blood'. Or take three ounces of onions, boil them in wine, give the patient to drink and then shout suddenly 'Be healed of thy issue'.

48

Then after twelve years she heard of a new presence in the locality and crowds swarming in from as far away as Transjordan with no other aim but touch him, and they were healed of all manner of ailments. Could she believe that she too could be healed? She became desperate. She must touch this extraordinary man. But how? Stamped as contagious she was forbidden by the strictest Rabbinic Law to mix in any crowd. Did not Leviticus 15.25 set out the restriction in black and white? She had read the verse a hundred times. But this man must be different. So she edged her way into the crowd pushing this way and that anxious to reach the most dense part of the crowd where he was sure to be. She stood on tip toe and craned her neck. Then she saw him, his headdress, his cloak or tallith with the four distinctive tassels at the hem. Clearly a Rabbi of a kind. Her moment had come. She could touch him but dare she risk it? Suppose she was discovered. Suppose someone barred her way and shouted 'Get out you unclean slut'. But the crowd was dense and these people were not locals. No one would know her. She would not be caught. She could creep up behind this striking man and touch his clothes. Not more; only a touch, a touch on a tassel. And wonderful! She would be healed. She knew it. She believed it. 'If I touch even his clothes I shall be cured.' And she was. Instantly. Completely. Her haemorrhage dried up. At once it dried up. She was clean, free, gloriously free. She had made contact with Jesus of Nazareth. This is who the man was.

We like this story even if we do draw the line at the miraculous cure but may be we can get round this with a theory of autosuggestion. The woman thought so deeply that she would be cured that she was. It was a case of psychosomatic healing. It illustrates what we have come to know now, the extraordinary power of the mind over the body. So we accept the story warming to a Jesus who seeks out the ailing and distressed in the community. It is what we do in our modern social service. No doubt we do with varying degrees of success. But is this the point of the story, to encourage us to seek out and succour the needy? But Jesus did not seek this woman at all. He did not even know she was there. He asked 'Who touched me?' All the initiative was on the part of the woman. All the contact was made by her. What this story is crying aloud to tell us is that there is in the world a healing presence if only we will make contact with it, namely the presence of the living God in the person of Christ. But this is largely ignored in contemporary life as having any contribution to make to our happiness, health and healing.

Recently I came across a report of a brand-new hospital erected on a housing estate. It was equipped with every modern device for efficient surgery and nursing but in the whole complex of impressive buildings there was not one single, even tiny, room reserved and equipped for spiritual ministration – no altar, no sacraments, no quiet place for meditation. When this was pointed out to the architect he said he had simply not thought about it.

Let me take up the woman's words again: 'If I touch even his clothes, I shall be cured', or, as in the Authorised Version, 'be made whole'. No doubt it would be splendid if all the Christians in our country were well-informed, Church-going and committed, whereas so much Christian practice appears as mere conformity, superficial, easily classified as 'folk religion' operating only at peak times like Christmas. But be careful how you write it off. The power of Christ is such that even if we only touch the exteriors of the faith in him we are the better for it. Healing through contact, simply through contact, is the first message of this story of the woman and her haemorrhage. The presence of the body of Christ is a healing presence and we do well to make contact with it. At the Holy Communion the priest says 'The body of our Lord Jesus Christ which was given for you preserve thy body and soul unto everlasting life'. And let me throw in this. If you know any parents with babies encourage them to bring them for baptism even if they are a bit muddled in mind about it. Remember the text: 'If I do but touch'. And if you turn up Mark, chapter 10, verse 13 in the New-Testament you will read how they brought children to Jesus for him to touch.

2 BELIEVING

Now the second part of the story. The woman knew in herself that she was cured when she touched, and Jesus knew in himself that someone had purposely touched him for healing. He also knew that healing power had proceeded from him to effect the cure. What he did not know was the identity of the one who touched. He was a real man with the limitations of a human being. He had to ask 'Who touched my clothes?' His disciples ever slow to grasp the stature of their Master counted it a ridiculous question. 'You see the crowds pressing upon you and yet you ask, "Who touched me?"' But Jesus was supersensitive to touching. There is touching and there is touching. We all know this. When a young woman is touched, even lightly, by the man she loves it does something to her. This woman's touching was different from the touching of the crowds. It was purposeful touching. It was faith touching. She had said to herself 'If I touch even his clothes *I shall be cured*'. Jesus responded at once to that kind of touching. It conveyed to her through him the power (*dunamis* in Greek) of God.

If we have imagination we can see him scanning the faces all around him. Who was it who touched differently? We can sense the silence. And then the woman emerged and fell at his feet covered with confusion. Jesus looked at her face stamped with fear. Trembling she blurted out her story—twelve years unclean! He listened. Then as she watched his face her fear slid away as had her haemorrhage. 'My daughter', he said (he did not often use the phrase), 'your faith (note, not your touch, your faith) has cured you. Go in peace free for ever of this trouble.'

3 CONFESSING

Compassionate action? Yes, but with a strong streak in it. Why not let the woman escape the embarrassing publicity? Why not let her slip into the anonymity the crowds offered? But Jesus was concerned for more than the present physical health for her. He was concerned for the years and years ahead of her life and for all the vicissitudes through which it would have to pass as with us all. She would need a strong faith to carry her through, and there was a danger that this sudden burst of her faith in him and his power would as quickly fade if it were not strengthened at once. For that confession of her faith was necessary, public confession, confession before people. We tend to lose what we hide and faith hidden can drift down into superstition. The danger for this woman was that in time she might come to think she had been healed by magic and that Jesus was a magical healer and not the one through whom the power of the living God operates.

I was reading recently of an art teacher who made it a rule for everyone in class that, when they had been studying a certain masterpiece in an art gallery, or anywhere else, they should never come away simply exclaiming about its colour, composition or overall beauty. They should describe to someone else exactly what they had seen. 'You do not know what you have experienced', he used to say, 'until you have put it into words for someone else to hear.' Jesus did not let this woman go till she had told 'the whole truth' about her experience.

So touching by itself is insufficient. Superficial contact with

51

Christian institutions by itself is insufficient either for individuals or for a community. There has to be a living faith in a living God openly expressed. At the humbler level Christians should not hide from their friends that they attend church on Sundays. Faith is not only for healing, it is for strong buoyant living through the storms of life. So is it stretching the imagination too far to say that because this woman believed *and confessed* she became a woman of stature in her comunity? People looked to her for consolation and support in their time of need. And Jesus was concerned for that community as well as for the woman which is why he did not let her slip away after her healing. He saw that she told all that had happened to her. Do not hide your faith. This is what this story is telling us.

11

FROM A DIFFERENT ANGLE

When the Lord saw her his heart went out to her.

LUKE 7.13 (NEB)

Some time ago I was looking at a painting of a fine house in extensive grounds that I thought I knew fairly well, but I did not recognize the place, it looked so different. But the artist was not incompetent and the picture was not a poor one; it was simply that the house had been depicted from a different angle and in a different light from that to which I had grown accustomed. Different people may perceive the same place in different ways and none of them may be wrong. This is especially true with respect to objects and places that are complex, and certainly in the case of persons. Indeed the greater the person the greater the complexity and therefore the greater the certainty that different observers will see a rather different picture of the same person.

You will not be surprised when I go on to say that the historical Jesus was and is viewed differently by different observers. What I have given so far in these sermons has been the view of St Mark, the writer of the first gospel, long neglected because it comes second in the four set out in our New Testaments, and is shorter, but now for a number of decades given the most extraordinary attention by all manner of writers and students. It is an austere piece of writing and it is not too much to say that the historical Jesus it portrays in its vivid word pictures with their firm lines and strong colours is itself austere. Indeed in the crucifixion narrative it is stark. Not surprisingly then some readers shy away from this Jesus. It may be that some listening to the opening sermons in this collection scarcely recognize the Jesus they thought they knew. He seemed so strong, authoritative and impatient of any interference: anything but a gentle Saviour.

But different people see the same person differently, and they are not wrong, especially if the person is a towering figure, and the historical Jesus was certainly that. We need not be taken aback, then, to discover that in the other New Testament gospels Jesus is

53

seen differently from the Jesus St Mark depicted. St Luke is a case in point, and remember he was an artist with words, which St Mark was not. He saw differently and his word pictures are different. It is to some of his pictures that now we turn.

1 ST LUKE'S PICTURES

St Luke's gospel opens with the baby Jesus in the manger, woolly sheep in the fields and angels in the sky singing 'Glory to God in the highest'. Is all this hard historical fact? Or do we see here St Luke beginning to introduce a gentler presentation of Jesus, Jesus as a Saviour, a picture absent from St Mark? His stories have tender touches and my guess is that St Luke was a tender man who saw with tender eyes. So he couldn't resist telling this story how Jesus, accompanied by his disciples and a large crowd (there were always crowds swaying around him in the early stages of his ministry), was approaching a village called Nain when his passage was blocked. Out from the narrow village entrance there issued a funeral procession flanked by another large crowd of mourners and villagers. They met head on. The bereaved was a woman, a widow, now bereft of her sole support and stay, her only son. Her heart was broken, tears streamed down her face. Jesus saw her and was deeply moved; 'his heart went out to her'. 'Do not weep', he said, and with that stepped forward and with his hand on the bier halted the procession. 'Young man, rise up', he said and the dead man sat up and began to speak. This was not all. 'Jesus gave him back to his mother.' Who in the face of this tenderness could fail to see the kind of person he was? And the woman had asked for nothing, had made no appeal, had shown no indication of even a spark of faith. Everything in this picture of Jesus turns on his spontaneous entry into the sorrowful plight of this nameless woman. She asked for nothing and she received more than she could ever have dared to hope for. But the historical Jesus was like that. This is what St Luke wanted us to know, and I guess that we who have read what he wrote can dare to believe that God is like that, grace and graciousness are his characteristics.

Turn the pages now to chapter 10 of St Luke's gospel and read his story of the Good Samaritan. I need not recount it. It comprises one of the passages in the gospels everyone knows. But here is my question: would not our modern news vendors have written up the horror of this wretched battered man by the roadside, stripped, beaten, half dead and robbed of his possessions? Jesus did not smooth over this ugliness but he left us with a lovely picture of how the man was succoured by a stranger turning up, a foreigner. 'The Good Samaritan' is the title of this picture, not 'the bloodthirsty muggers'. Jesus drew attention to the good things that do exist even in a rough world. He was like that and St Luke wanted us to see this characteristic of Jesus because that is what he himself saw.

2 THREE PARABLES

And now three more pictures – the three parables of the lost sheep, the lost coin and the lost son. Wonderful pictures they are of God's concern for any or all of us who have lost our way in life. But come down to earth. From where did Jesus derive these stories? From books? From fables? From his own fertile imagination? Let me make a suggestion. One day he saw with his own eyes a local shepherd wringing his hands in anguish because one of his precious sheep had broken out of the pen. The man was nearly in tears. He must find that sheep, and there was no ravine too steep, no thicket too dense, no lair of wild beasts he would not search to find that precious but lost sheep. And he did find it. You should have seen his face when he came back home with his sheep around his shoulders! Jesus saw him and, note this, he felt, yes he felt for him and the whole tender sight came out in his parable. He identified with the shepherd. He put himself in the shepherd's shoes, he was like that.

Then that other day when passing the open door of a house he watched a woman with a lamp in her hand sweeping every corner and crevice of her room searching anxiously, perhaps with tears in her eyes, for a lost piece of silver, broken away maybe from her necklace. But she found it and then woman-like she called together her friends and neighbours to break the good news. A trivial domestic scene? Yes, of course but Jesus noticed it because he could sense anguish whenever it occurred. He knew how a woman would feel, yes a woman, at the loss of something precious to her. He was like that. So the incident found its way into his parable and St Luke warmed to it and wrote it in his gospel showing how he saw Jesus.

And who could forget that poor father, day after day never able to take his eyes off the high road by which his wayward son had left to live his wastrel life far from home? Would he come back? He did come back in rags and emaciated, but repentant. And the father, not much given to dancing at the best of times, danced for

55

joy, and laid on the best welcome-home party he could devise. Perhaps Jesus was one of the guests. I put it like this because I suggest – I can only suggest – that Jesus saw all this happen and was happy as one of the party. He was like that. All this came out in the parable we call the Prodigal Son which we tend to classify as fiction. Perhaps it is, but most fiction has a basis in fact.

3 TENDERNESS AND SEVERITY

I could go on. I could tell of Jesus, happy in the home of two women Martha and Mary, each giving him pleasure by what they each had to contribute to the occasion, different from each other as they were. I could tell of the women who clubbed together their resources to provide for the bodily needs of Jesus and his disciples. I could tell of the women who openly wept as they saw Jesus goaded along the ghastly road that led to the crucifixion site, the *via dolorosa*, bearing the incriminatory placard 'Jesus of Nazareth the King of the Jews'. He was sorry for these women, not for himself, and bade them dry their eyes. St Luke's gospel more than any other shows how Jesus was sensitive to women.

This is what I want to say. You and I have not seen the real Jesus, the historical Jesus, Jesus with a face, unless we have looked hard and long at St Luke's pictures in his gospel as well as St Mark's austere representations. There was a tender side to his manhood which women in particular were quick to recognize. Make no mistake however, he wasn't soft. Listen to this also from St Luke's gospel, the words of Jesus: 'Alas for you, Chorazin! Alas for you, Bethsaida! If the miracles that were performed in you had been performed in Tyre and Sidon, they would have repented long ago, sitting in sackcloth and ashes. But it will be more bearable for Tyre and Sidon at the Judgement than for you. And as for you, Capernaum, will you be exalted to the skies? No, brought down to the depths!' Stinging words! but Jesus could be like that when it came to religious superficiality and hypocrisy; and not only religious, but political as well. He could strip off people's masks and show up their ugly faces underneath.

4 CHECK YOUR PICTURE OF JESUS

How shall I conclude this sermon? If you profess to be a Christian, a believing Christian, you will have your own picture of Jesus, indeed having it will be an indication that you are in truth a Christian. Your picture may be different from mine and from your neighbour's. This is inevitable, but the point I want to leave with you, and why I have preached this sermon (and this whole series) is that you and I must check our picture from time to time with the picture that is given in the gospels. This checking will bring us closer to the real Jesus and this is important because it is in him that *God is made known*, or as St Paul wrote in his letter to the Christians of Corinth, 'Seeing it is God, that said, Light shall shine out of darkness, who shone in our hearts, to give the light of the knowledge of the glory of God in *the face of Jesus Christ*' (2 Corinthians 4.6 RV).

12

THE JESUS WHO FORGIVES SINS

*Then he (Jesus) said to her, 'Your sins are forgiven'. The other guests
began to ask themselves, 'Who is this, that he can forgive sins?' But
he said to the woman, 'Your faith has saved you; go in peace'.*

LUKE 7.48 (NEB)

Who is this woman? We don't know. No name is given. But Simon
the Pharisee knew, and a number of other men also knew, for she
lived 'an immoral life in the town' as the New English Bible
delicately describes her. Bluntly speaking she was a prostitute, or
had been, plying her trade probably in Capernaum, where a con-
tingent of Roman soldiers was billeted under the command of a
centurion. Probably Jesus had seen her on the streets, for Capernaum was where he himself lived and in and out of which he conducted his itinerant ministry in Galilee. Doubtless she had seen
him. I suggest that she was powerfully attracted to him—he was
attractive—and maybe crept into the Capernaum synagogue to hear
him preach. What she heard affected her deeply. We shall come to
this later.

1 THE EMBARRASSING DEMONSTRATION

First we turn our attention to a Pharisee called Simon. Unlike the
woman he was eminently respectable, it would be fair to say 'a good
man'. So he is given a name. For reasons unknown he invited Jesus
to dinner, a brave act on his part for the members of his party were
consistently hostile to Jesus. But was curiosity his motive? Was it
that he wondered how an erstwhile carpenter from Nazareth would
show up in a social setting? Was this invitation even a subtle device
to humiliate Jesus in company and put him in his place, as it were?
We don't know. But other guests were present. They entered the
room more or less together and slipping in was this woman.

Noting the place at table where Jesus was reclining in customary fashion, his feet out from the table, and bereft of sandals, she took up a position immediately behind him at his feet. This proximity to him was too much for her emotions. She broke down in copious tears, so copious they wetted his feet. Overcome, she shook out her hair and wiped them. And if this was not enough she kissed them again and again. (The Greek word here is distinctive, it means fervently or affectionately.) Nor was this even the end of her demonstration. Producing a small flask of oil of myrrh, clearly brought on purpose, she proceeded to anoint his feet. Oil of myrrh was expensive only used on special occasions. When Naomi in the Old Testament story instructed Ruth to seek out her kinsman Boaz she bade her anoint herself in preparation. Simon the Pharisee was horrified by this exhibition of feminine devotion at his table; it was vulgar, it was coarse; respectable women did not loose their hair in public. 'Ah, I thought so', he said to himself, 'if this fellow were a real prophet he would know who this woman is that touched him, and what sort of woman she is, a sinner.'

So had Simon invited Jesus to his table to try him out? Nothing was said, but Jesus took him up showing that, far from Simon reading him, he was reading Simon. In magisterial fashion, almost with a touch of irony he addressed his host directly, calling him by name, 'Simon, I have something to say to you'. 'Speak on, Master' came the reply. Was there a slight shrug of the shoulders? It matters little what you say. I have seen with my own eyes all I need to know. There came a little parable on Jesus' lips, a very little parable. 'Two men were in debt to a moneylender; one owed him five hundred pieces of silver, the other fifty. As neither had anything to pay with he let them both off. Now which will love him the most?' Simon replied 'I should think the one who was let off most'. It was the obvious answer.

We may guess that the room fell silent. All eyes were on Jesus. Slowly and deliberately he turned for the first time in the whole incident to face the woman but still addressing Simon, 'You see this woman?' Simon certainly saw her, he scarcely saw anyone else. 'I came to your house: you provided no water for my feet; but this woman has made my feet wet with her tears and wiped them with her hair. You gave me no kiss (that is the perfunctory kiss of greeting on the cheek) but she has been kissing my feet (the Greek word meaning fervently or affectionately) since I came in. You did not anoint my head with oil (olive oil plentiful and relatively cheap in Palestine) but she has anointed my feet with myrrh. And so, I tell you, her great love proves that her many sins have been forgiven; where little has been forgiven, little love is shown.' Then,

59

no doubt still looking at the woman, he said to her, 'Your sins are forgiven'. She knew this of course, which was why she had sought out Jesus' presence. Was there a murmur at this point among the other guests at table? 'Who is this, that can forgive sins?' So the question that would not go away, the question about the identity of Jesus. 'But he said to the woman "Your faith has saved you; go in peace".' She would need no second bidding. As quickly and unobtrusively as she had slipped in to this Pharisaic company she would slip out. Jesus remained. The guests remained. What were they thinking? What was Simon thinking? What are we thinking?

2 RECEIVING FORGIVENESS

I feel bound to comment warmly on the translation which the New English Bible provides at this point in the story. I am glad, and not least because I cannot say that the literary quality is always of a high standard, though sometimes more enlightening of the meaning of the passage of scripture. What I note here are the words 'And so, I tell you, her great love proves that her many sins have been forgiven'. The case is not that her great love earned for her the forgiveness of sins. No one can earn forgiveness. It is a free gift to be accepted or not. What I think happened was that this woman was attracted by Jesus and I include here what she had heard of him and how he turned his back on no one whatever they had said or done, or what had befallen them by way of illness or deprivation. Perhaps she had seen him in action with the maimed and diseased in and around Capernaum, and then when she heard him proclaim the forgiveness of God to all who truly repent for what they have done—was it perhaps in the Capernaum synagogue?—she opened her heart to the message and felt that forgiveness sweep over her filling her whole being with an extraordinary peace. How could she ever thank God? How could she thank the man who conveyed the message? She could not make speeches. And anyway how could she make contact with the man, she of all people with her past? But she was a woman. Love was her medium. She would find a way, and she did. She found the money to buy that small flask of oil of myrrh. She would pour it on his feet. The action would say all. That dinner party with Simon the Pharisee provided the opportunity. She slipped in with the guests and if her emotions did get the better of her she had shown her love, the outcome of the forgiveness she knew she had in the secret of her soul. But she heard it out loud at this dinner table from the lips of Jesus himself: 'Your sins are forgiven.' The others reclining there might raise questions about who could forgive sins, but not this woman. She knew the answer. She crept away 'on air', the words ringing in her ears, 'Your faith has saved you; go in peace'. All that happened to her happened because she had believed the message and trusted the messenger. And what came back to her, we may be sure, was the dignity of her womanhood which she had besmirched and men had besmirched. She could lift up her head.

Some time ago I read of a clergyman crossing Trafalgar Square in London. He was dressed in clerical clothes and looked very respectable. Surprisingly, or perhaps not surprisingly, a prostitute sidling up to him offered her services, man of the cloth though he was, but still a man. What happened all but overwhelmed her, and she told the story afterwards, indeed the incident changed her life. Politely he raised his hat to her, smiled, and said kindly 'No, thank you'. She might have expected an insult – 'Get out, you filthy little slut', but the treatment of her as a woman worthy of respect restored to her what she had lost. Something like this is behind the story we have been considering of the woman who came to anoint Jesus as he reclined at table in Simon the Pharisee's house.

3 SIMON THE PHARISEE

And now the little parable which Jesus told on this occasion. Do you remember it? 'Two men were in debt to a money-lender: one owed him five hundred silver pieces, the other fifty. As neither had anything to pay with he let them both off. Now which will love him most?' What I ask you to notice is 'he let them *both* off'. Very well. We have been considering the woman. She experienced the forgiveness of her sins. Categorically Jesus declared her forgiveness. We like this. We warm to it. But don't overlook the statement in the parable – he *let them both off*. So there was forgiveness for the Pharisee as well as for the woman, forgiveness for Simon.

When I began this sermon I half suggested that this Pharisee might have invited Jesus to dinner with some ulterior motive, perhaps to trap him in some way. We don't know why he issued the invitation but Jesus accepted it. Simon, for his part, accepted Jesus into his house, which is not insignificant. All this acts as a reminder that not all the Pharisees were bad and how we must be careful at all times not to write people off in bulk. There were good

Pharisees and bad Pharisees and Simon was one of the former. He wasn't perfect, he wasn't anything like a saint. He had some blots on his character, but he had not sunk anything like so far down the side of respectability as had the woman with her small flask of myrrh. But he needed forgiveness too and it was available for him as for her, as was the peace which is the consequence. I can't help wondering if that simple receiving of Jesus on Simon's part in spite of the apparent omissions in his style of receiving was not the avenue along which God's mercy and forgiving grace could come to him. This is the point. If we shut ourselves off from Jesus nothing can come to us from God via him, but if we open our door but a tiny way, blessing will come. Is there not that other story in the gospels where the woman with a haemorrhage said 'If I touch even his clothes I shall be cured', and she was? Could Simon the Pharisee have said to himself 'If I even invite him into my house I shall be made clean'? Let me repeat what I said about Jesus' little parable of the two debtors. There was forgiveness, apparently, for the Pharisee.

Reading through the gospels in the New Testament I see that Jesus did not elaborate on the doctrine of the forgiveness of sins. His hearers generally were Jews familiar with prophetic utterances about God's forgiveness of sin and the elaborate priestly system which made ritual provision for it. What Jesus brought was a revelation of the friendly face of God who cared for sinners whether Pharisees or women on the streets. That kindly, attractive face of Jesus, turning people towards God instead of away from God. The face was one of the first instruments in his ministry, it is always in with every minister of the gospel for good or ill, for attraction or repelling. Both Simon and the woman with the small flask of myrrh liked the look of Jesus. That is the stage at which they started their spiritual pilgrimage, lowly but real.

One more point – repentance and turning away from the kind of life the woman had lived on the streets is necessary. Sin is not glossed over in the economy of God. And the Pharisee must surrender his spiritual pride if the peace of God is to be experienced. You are not likely to forget the woman in this story from St Luke chapter 7, it is a masterpiece, but don't forget Simon the Pharisee. Be careful how you judge the Simons you meet. I must be careful too, mustn't I?

13

THE EASING OF BURDEN

'Come to me, all whose work is hard, whose load is heavy; and I will give you relief. Bend your necks to my yoke, and learn from me, for I am gentle and humble-hearted; and your souls will find relief. For my yoke is good to bear, my load is light.'

MATTHEW 11.28–30 (NEB)

Or in the familiar words of that lovely soprano aria in Handel's *Messiah*: 'Come unto me all ye that labour and are heavy laden and I will give you rest. Take my yoke upon you and learn of me for I am meek and lowly in heart and ye shall find rest into your souls. For my yoke is easy and my burden is light.'

First a brief word of explanation about the yoke. It has been said that Jesus used to make yokes in his carpenter's shop before he became a preacher, and there was a sign over his premises which read 'My yokes are easy'. Maybe. I don't know but I can tell you that the plough in Palestine was normally drawn by a pair of small red oxen over whose back a yoke was cast. It consisted of a light beam of wood and was fastened under the animal's neck by leather straps. It was easy to bear if the wood was light and the animals yoked together were of about equal size. Jesus invited his hearers to share his yoke for it would give them relief in the task of bearing the heavy loads of life.

1 RULES AND REGULATIONS

His hearers must have pricked up their ears. They knew only too well what a burden religion could be as presented by the authorities of their day. The rules and regulations ran into hundreds. A man had to watch his every step to make sure he wasn't contravening some ordinance. Then one day in a swingeing frontal attack on those very authorities Jesus said

The scribes and the Pharisees sit on Moses' seat: all things therefore whatsoever they bid you, these do and observe: but do not after their works for they say and do not. Yea, they bind heavy burdens and grievous to be borne, and lay them on men's shoulders: but they themselves will not move them with their finger. (Matthew 23.2−4 RV)

What he was attacking was religion which consists of rules and regulations. Judaism at its worst became that and Christianity can become that too. Understandably we shy off it. There are burdens enough in life without adding religious ones. But make no mistake, there have to be moral standards; there have to be guidelines for conduct. We cannot with impunity abolish the Ten Commandments, and you can be certain Jesus did not write them off. If however we make rules and regulations the be-all and end-all of our religion we shall fail miserably to derive any uplift from it. Jesus presented religion of a different kind. Its spring of action, and it had a spring of action, lay elsewhere. It lay in love, love of God and love of neighbour.

There came a day when Jesus made this plain. Not that the Jews did not know it. Every day they recited what is generally called the *Shema* (because of the opening words in Hebrew, 'Hear O Israel'), but a routine can become perfunctory and its application to life be lost. Sadly, this is what had happened in Judaism in Jesus' time. One day however Jesus was engaged in a sharp altercation with the Jewish sect, the Sadducees, who did not believe in the resurrection. His retort on that occasion silenced them but one of the Pharisees, the sect which did believe it, decided to test him out, perhaps with his tongue in his cheek, 'Master, which is the greatest commandment in the law?' Did Jesus smile then at the naïveté of the trap laid for him? His reply was almost a recitation: 'Love the Lord your God with all your heart, with all your soul, with all your mind. That is the greatest commandment. It comes first. The second is like it, Love your neighbour as yourself. Everything in the Law and the prophets hangs on these two commandments' (Matthew 22.34−39). I should like to have seen that Pharisee's face as he walked away. There was simply nothing to say.

2 THE ESSENCE OF TRUE RELIGION

But we shall be wise not to walk away but rather grasp that the religion which Jesus taught was the expression of two commandments only based on one disposition−love. It was as simple as that, and as demanding. It was not a religion of rules and regulations grievous to be borne. All the same, how is it possible to achieve this basic requirement, how can we love God? We have never seen him. The God however whom Jesus revealed in his words and deeds was in fact easy to love because they radiated love, love of people of all kinds, even strangers, even people broken and maimed and diseased. No one was a reject. The God whom Jesus revealed was more like a kindly neighbour, a compassionate friend. This is the impression the ordinary people of Judaea and Galilee gained from watching the historical Jesus, Jesus with a face. If then the essence of true religion is to love *this God* what a load it lifted off their minds and spirits, and off our mind and spirits. Matthew 11 verses 28 to 30 says it all. 'Come to me, all who labour and are heavy laden, and I will give you rest. Take my yoke upon you, and learn from me; for I am gentle and lowly in heart, and you will find rest for your souls.'

There is one necessity however for this to be realized, we have to 'see' Jesus. We cannot love what we do not see. But we can see. We see by reading the gospels in the New Testament. And if there is also preaching of the historical Jesus, making him come alive as a person, how fortunate we are. There is the clear possibility for us to love him with all our heart, all our soul and with all our mind, and our neighbour as ourselves. This is good news. It brings true religion, uplifting religion, buoyant religion, energizing religion within our grasp, ordinary people though we be. This then is the gospel of the historical Jesus. This is why he must be preached. Our salvation lies in warming to him. What a simple gospel this is! How wide open to us all!

3 THE GOSPEL OF REST

And now this word 'rest'. 'Come unto me all ye that labour and are heavy laden and I will give you rest': the word used here in the Greek is *anapausis*. It means uplift. The picture is of someone weighed down, even sagging, with a load of luggage, hardly able to crawl along, stopping every now and then for breath. And someone turns up not to take the load away altogether, but to give relief from its weight, to make possible the carrying of it, so that the journey can be continued. It is rather like some wretched traveller carrying his luggage in two huge handbags, the weight of which all but tears both his arms out of their sockets. And then someone provides him with a rucksack. The luggage still has to be carried, but the carrying is made easier than he ever thought possible by being transferred to the rucksack, taking the weight off his arms and legs on to his back. What a relief!

We all have some luggage to lug along in life, some people more than others. For large numbers of people in the modern world it is anxiety about the future. Shall I be made redundant in my job? Can I keep up my mortgage payments? What is happening about my son's or daughter's marriage? And this nagging pain in my chest? And you look at me, the preacher, as if I have gone off my head. What on earth, you complain, has religion to do with such situations as these? Religion can't make jobs! No, but it can ease the burden of anxiety which these situations so easily cause. We can commit our fears to God and we can trust in his care of us as a heavenly Father. Yes, I know, we can write this off as trite, no more than religious claptrap, the kind of thing it is supposed preachers are paid to say, but it works. There is another wonderful aria in an oratorio: 'Cast thy burden upon the Lord and he shall sustain thee.' How is it that some men and women carry on through back-breaking difficulties, even with cheerfulness? The answer is they do not carry it all themselves they share it with God who, they trust, cares for them. One of the most striking traits about the historical Jesus is his unhurried serenity, even up to that horrible crucifixion. *Angst* is what the Germans call our perpetual worrying about life. Committing this burden to God will help lighten this load. It is what Jesus did and the resultant equipoise was impressive.

Then there is that burden of past mistakes, some of them down-right sinful. We can't forget them. They dog us, drag us down; and the more sensitive we are the heavier they weigh upon us. But God is ready and willing to forgive and then we can forgive ourselves. Frequently we read in the gospels how Jesus spoke a word of forgiveness to individuals and out of this release came the power to go on again with a life not crippled by the past.

For some men and women there is the burden of personal deficiencies. They are not as capable as some of their friends and neighbours. They know they can never 'make it to the top'. They lack distinctive skills. And some have a deformity. Others are 'slow in the uptake', as we say. Ordinary defects, no doubt, but they weigh people down in comparison with the ease and success of others. They may come to the point of bitterly resenting them. What is necessary is to accept that we are as we are and the God who cares knows all about us. The historical Jesus turned away from no one. So we can see what God is like and if as a result of watching him we can let go our burden of resentment, yes and inferiority complex, we can lift up our heads and walk upright in the world, *anapausis* is the Greek word, uplift. 'Come unto me' said Jesus 'and I will give you rest.' There is a gospel (good news) of rest to be found as we respond to the historical Jesus as set out by St Matthew in chapter 11, verses 28 to 30, so different, so utterly different from the religion of rules and regulations which has put off so many people in so many times.

In Charles Dickens' novel *The Old Curiosity Shop* is a story of a poor old man not only enfeebled but dogged by a gambling mania. Dogged and tricked by his landlords, his granddaughter, Nell, saw that there was no hope for them trying to maintain their dwindling business: they had to get away. So they did, the two of them together, the young woman supporting the old man. They had no idea what their destination was to be. They only knew they must get away. So they tramped across fields and passed through villages, living and sleeping rough. Some people whom they encountered were kind, some were not. As was to be expected, the old man could go no further and his granddaughter feared for the worst. Then out of the blue came help from a schoolmaster who offered them shelter and provisions, a striking illustration of the text: 'Come unto me all you that labour and are heavy laden and I will give you rest.'

In these sermons we began by noting the historical Jesus whom St Mark saw, authoritative and strong. And the way in which St Luke saw him, compassionate and tender. Today in this sermon we are likely to fasten on the words St Matthew reported of him: 'For I am meek and lowly in heart and you shall find rest into your souls', or as the New English Bible has it 'for I am gentle and humble-hearted; and your souls will find relief'. All because his yoke is easy—yes, there is a yoke but it is light to bear. It is the same Jesus whom all three gospel writers portrayed. Different people saw him differently, but what each saw was true. You and I are different from each other and from the man and woman next door but we shall all find what we each need in the God revealed in the historical Jesus. We shall be wise to ally ourselves to him, that is take upon ourselves his easy yoke and lean on him. We shall find our burdens uplifted, we shall find rest into our souls.

14

THE BREAD OF LIFE

'There is a boy here who has five barley loaves and two fishes; but what is that among so many?' Jesus said, 'Make the people sit down'. There was plenty of grass there, so the men sat down, about five thousand of them. Then Jesus took the loaves, gave thanks, and distributed them to the people as they sat there. He did the same with the fishes, and they had as much as they wanted.

JOHN 6.9–11 (NEB)

The subject of this sermon is Jesus as the bread of life based on the story of the feeding of five thousand people with five barley loaves and two small fishes – some would label it a 'tall story'. I can't omit this incident in preaching on the historical Jesus because it marked a crisis in his ministry and has the rare distinction of being recorded in all four gospels. I have already made brief reference to it in an earlier sermon but it calls for fuller treatment.

1 THE BOY

Guided by the text from John 6.9 I begin with the boy. 'There is a boy here who has five barley loaves and two fishes.' He has always captivated my imagination. I wrote briefly about him in my book published by the Bible Reading Fellowship entitled *God's Masterpieces* and am unable to prevent some of the descriptive phrases used there creeping into this sermon, indeed some repetition is unavoidable. The boy then. My guess, and of course it is only a guess, is that his mother had sent him out for the day having packed up his picnic – five barley loaves, the kind of bread the poor ate, and two dainty little fishes to compensate for their dryness. He wandered along as boys do and joined up with a crowd which seemed to be moving in one direction, and soon found himself on a hill near the lake of Galilee listening to a man preaching. There was plenty of grass there so the time must have been early spring.

68

He sat down to listen holding on tight, we may be sure, to his packed lunch. No one moved. They seemed spellbound. They were in fact still sitting there as darkness was beginning to fall.

Then something embarrassing happened. A man came up to him and asked for his picnic, yes, all five barley buns and the two tiny fishes, and ushered him up to the preacher. He did not know what to say. But there was no need to say anything. No one standing around said anything. Instead they all looked puzzled. They gave the impression that they thought the preacher did not understand the enormity of the situation. This huge crowd, darkness soon to fall, no shops nearby, and everyone desperate for a bite of something; and there was this boy thrust forward with five buns and two little fishes! Could any situation be more absurd—indeed laughable—if they were not so worried about the consequences? Five thousand people and a boy with five barley loaves and two little fishes.

Then the boy gave the preacher his five buns and two dainty fishes. And the preacher took them, looked up to heaven, as the account says, gave thanks (Greek *eucharistēsas*: I shall come to that later) and distributed them with the assistance of his disciples to the people as they sat there. He did the same with the fishes. And all had as much as they wanted.

2 ESSENTIALLY A MIRACLE

This is the point at which many people switch off and maybe we switch off. Five buns cannot be multiplied to feed five thousand people. It is contrary to natural law and therefore impossible. A first lesson in science is that matter cannot be created, neither can it be destroyed. I had that dinned into my head when I was fourteen, so perhaps did you. Somehow then we have to get round this story. Shall we say that what happened was that the crowd, seeing the boy was willing to give up his picnic, brought out the food they had hidden away on their persons and shared it with their neighbours sitting on the grass, and the whole five thousand were fed? The miracle was the crowd's willingness to share their possessions. But was it? This explanation raises bigger problems. Whatever it was that happened—and let us be honest, we don't know exactly—the crowd was so thrilled at the possibilities it held for feeding the nation that it made an attempt to seize Jesus and make him king. What could he not do for the whole country? Now I ask you, would such enthusiasm have been engendered by a shared picnic? Or many shared secreted food supplies? Also this: if you extract all miracle from the event you render the story commonplace, and then it has no *religious* value. Why bother with it? Indeed why record it? What we all want deep down inside us is the knowledge of some power *beyond* the ordinary, beyond the weakness, fragility and fallibility of life as we know it. We need God in his love and almighty power, and if religion does not put us in touch with him, it has little or no value, why bother with it?

Someone may suggest another way out. This story of the feeding of the five thousand is a legend, someone made it up. But there are four accounts of this event, and while it is obvious they all describe the same event they don't exactly tally. Now there can't have been *four legends* invented nearly all alike but with significant differences! What must be behind these four accounts are a number of stories derived from eyewitnesses. The overall agreements together with the slight differences point to an historical event. The stubborn fact is that we cannot by means of *adjustment* make this story acceptable. We have to accept it or reject it, but if we accept it, hard questions are raised about the identity of Jesus – who really was he? – as in the case of the other outstanding nature miracle (so-called) the stilling of the storm, when the disciples asked 'Who can this be whom even the wind and sea obey?'

3 THREE SIMPLE LESSONS

I have been raising intricate questions and you may be wondering if there are not simpler lessons to be learned from this story. I think there are and the first is that Jesus fed these people because he saw they were hungry. It was as simple as that. He felt for them. Darkness was coming on and there were no shops nearby where purchases might be made. And what about the women and the children present? They were a long way from home. Jesus is concerned for *human physical needs*, and those who are his disciples must keep in the forefront of their activities strenuous efforts to relieve poverty, want and deprivation. There are parts of the world where the need for this cries aloud. Relief work is nothing less than following in the footsteps of the historical Jesus. We must never forget this. It is a basic Christian lesson.

Secondly, come back to the little boy and his picnic. I find him attractive. He gave his little, five barley buns, and with it Jesus fed five thousand people. In the German New Testament is a charming line drawing of him and underneath these words which I will translate as follows: 'so little you have to offer—so much when Christ passes it on'. Surely you, as a Christian man or woman, must have said to yourself 'There is so little I can do to forward the Christian gospel and way of life. I can't preach. I can't be an evangelist. I can't organize campaigns, arrange rallies, knock on people's doors.' But you can be seen attending church. You can refuse to hide from your friends and associates at work that you are a churchgoer. You can adhere to the life-style that testifies to your Christian allegiance. It takes courage especially in the workplace. When in Rome it is hard not to do as Rome does. 'Only a little', you say, but the boy gave his little and Jesus multiplied it to feed the multitudes in such a surprising, even inexplicable way, that we can scarcely believe it. So little you have to offer, but it can be so much when Christ takes it and uses it. This is the message of the boy with five barley buns and two dainty fishes. Don't forget the boy!

Thirdly, the crowds were not pleased that Jesus escaped their effort to make him king on the spot, so thrilled were they with his marvellous provision of bread to eat in a desert place. It was like the manna Moses gave the Israelites, their forebears, in the wilderness after the exodus from Egypt. Jesus however did not intend his ministry to stop at the provision of bread for the hungry, important as this was to him. He was concerned with spiritual food, food for the soul without which life deteriorates. So next morning in the Capernaum synagogue he preached on the bread of life. Only one gospel, that of St John, tells of this and that of necessity in summary form, drawing out the inner meaning of what Jesus meant: 'I am the living bread which has come down from heaven; if anyone eats this bread he shall live for ever' though the actual wording may be St John's. In reading St John's gospel we must be ready for this interpretative way of writing. We are to understand the crowds got the message, and they didn't like it. Yes the provision of bread was fine but not this sort of spiritual bread. At this point in the ministry the crowds hitherto much in evidence faded away. Even the twelve disciples were shaken but they kept faith. A climax had been reached. From now on the death at Jerusalem was never far from Jesus' mind.

Before we leave this scene we must allow ourselves to be reminded of the Eucharistic Christian worship. In the Upper Room on the night before his crucifixion Jesus took bread, gave thanks (Greek *eucharistēsas*) and gave it to his disciples; and near Bethsaida where

71

he fed the five thousand he took five barley loaves, gave thanks and distributed to the people who sat there waiting. So wrote John in his gospel. Since he did not include an account of the last supper it is hard not to think that he intended this feeding of the five thousand to be not only a feeding of the bodily hungry but as feeding sacramentally, feeding with the bread of life. So the words in John 6.35: 'I am the bread of life. Whoever comes to me shall never be hungry, and whoever believes in me shall never be thirsty.'

15

THE TURNING-POINT

'Who do men say I am?'

MARK 8.27 (NEB)

It is unlikely there is anyone in this congregation above the age of 25 who does not understand what is meant by a turning-point in life. You look back and see that your leaving home to be on your own was a turning-point, perhaps your first job, entry into college or university, maybe living in lodgings and meeting at close quarters all manner of new people, some you liked and some you heartily disliked. Looking back you can see that that break with your accustomed background was a turning-point in your life. Thereafter you began to be a rather different person. Marriage is another turning-point, and the arrival of the first child, and the day when husband and wife are on their own again, the children having grown up and left home to make their own way in their world. Yes, we understand what a turning-point in life means.

In my sermon today I propose drawing your attention to the period of two turning-points in the life of Jesus, the first being when he closed the carpenter's shop door in Nazareth for the last time, said goodbye to his family and set out for the Jordan river for the start of his ministry of preaching and healing in Galilee. Some of his deeds and words we have been considering in this series of sermons. His was an intensely active life always beset by clamorous crowds, always in the public eye, frequently misunderstood, sometimes in danger. It is this part of his ministry most people know about if they know anything about Jesus at all—the miracles, the parables, the choice of the twelve disciples, the confrontations with the religious authorities. This however is only part of his ministry, the Galilean part. There came a turning-point after which he left Galilee never to return, and there developed a different kind of ministry altogether. This was part two, the training of the twelve disciples preparing them for what he knew was coming and they did not—his crucifixion. The turning-point was at a place called Caesarea Philippi. Let me tell you about it.

Caesarea Philippi, so called to distinguish it from the Caesarea

73

on the Mediterranean coast, was a beautifully situated town on a plateau to the north of the Galilean lake made especially significant by nestling at the foot of the spectacular snow-capped mountain, Hermon. Originally called Paneas because of the local shrine dedicated to the heathen god Pan, it had been built up by Herod Philip and named after the Roman Emperor Caesar Augustus, hence the name Caesarea Philippi. Remote therefore not only in location but in culture from Galilee with its Jewish background and tensions, for it was Greek and therefore Gentile territory. Jesus chose to go into the countryside there for the seclusion it offered and the opportunity to raise with his disciples two fundamentals, namely the question of his identity: Who really was he? And to announce his forthcoming crucifixion. This then was the great turning-point of his ministry. Jesus we are told prepared for it with prayer as he did for that other momentous occasion when he chose his twelve disciples.

1 THE GREAT QUESTION

Now the question which marks the turning-point. Where exactly it was asked is not clear. Was it on the road to the village of Caesarea Philippi, as St Mark says, or when Jesus was praying alone there with his disciples, as St Luke says? What is clear is the question itself: 'Who do men say I am?' He was not seeking information but using it to introduce the really crucial question: 'Who do *you* say I am?' The various answers about public opinion show how much he was talked about, some comments serious and thoughtful, others light-hearted no doubt and flippant. In general however Jesus was popularly seen as a top-ranking prophet on a level with the great ones of Israel. John the Baptist come back again was one idea, another Elijah or Jeremiah, instigated by the general belief that the advent of the Messiah would be preceded by the appearance of one such giant of the past. What is interesting is the *variety* of names suggested. To some people Jesus looked like John the Baptist the powerful rousing preacher, to others he looked like Elijah the national warrior on behalf of the true God, to others Jeremiah the sensitive and retiring yet faithful witness to an apostate nation. Clearly Jesus was a many-sided man capturing attention from widely diverse groups in the community, indicating a kind of universality about him. In general the names given him indicate how highly most people ranked him. There were those however who had other names for him. They called him a Samaritan, a popular form of abuse on the lips of Jews. They labelled him a devil, a madman, a drunkard, a friend of the riffraff of society. These were the religious authorities who counted him a dangerous rival.

Now I suggest, and it can be more than a suggestion, that there was a momentary pause, the great question was about to be asked, the great turning-point in Jesus' ministry had come. Did he hold his breath? Did the faces of the twelve disciples indicate the tenseness of the occasion? The question could not be suppressed any longer. It must come out, at least for the disciples. It is a question which has never gone away and never will go away. It has been asked by every generation of men and women since that day at Caesarea Philippi. It is still being asked in books, conversations, discussion groups, and by the media. 'Who do you say I am?' Who do you say Jesus is, the historical Jesus? We do well to pause before we answer.

2 THE GREAT ANSWER

Peter among the twelve disciples did not pause. He was not given to pausing before he spoke. He reacted more to promptings of his heart, than reasoning in his head. For a long time he had been feeling, that is the word, feeling, that there was something different about this teacher, something massively different. Perhaps that occasion when the disciples in the boat thought they must all be drowned in that frightening storm on the lake when suddenly the howling winds and the lashing waves subsided and the disciples in the boat, mystified, asked themselves 'Who then is this that the winds and the sea obey him?' And that stunning feeding of the five thousand people when they had only five loaves at their disposal. Far however from calling attention to his extraordinary powers, Jesus appeared reluctant to use them and even anxious to suppress excited talk about them. Totally unlike leaders, out to make a name, he evinced no display whatsoever. He was therefore an enigma, but an intriguing enigma, they knew no measuring rod by which to assess him. Peter however at Caesarea Philippi on a sudden inspiration spoke up in answer to Jesus' enquiry, 'Who do *you* say I am?' 'You are the Messiah' (Mark 8.29) or as St Matthew words his answer, 'You are the Christ, the Son of the living God' (Matthew 16.16). And then this extraordinary command: he, Jesus, gave them strict orders not to tell anyone about him.

Most of us who give the name 'Christ' to Jesus do so almost automatically. We have grown accustomed to its usage, perhaps even accept it as a kind of surname following the forename Jesus. And many people dodging the name Jesus as sounding too pietistic fall back on 'Christ' as more non-committal. A few people there are who,

75

having given thought to the whole matter, use the name 'Jesus' when they wish specifically to refer to the historical Jesus who walked about in Galilee and Judaea nearly two thousand years ago, calling him perhaps 'Jesus of Nazareth' as did his contemporaries. No disrespect is implied. No underrating of his influence as a teacher in world history, no unwillingness to consider his healing, even his miraculous powers seriously. The distinctive fact about Peter's confession is that it was drawn out of him, out of his heart, out of his very being. After watching Jesus over a period of time in close association wondering, perhaps doubting, and then wondering again, and at last bursting out with the words 'You are the Christ, You are the Messiah', which later came to be filled out with the phrase 'the Son of the living God'.

How did the other eleven disciples react to this confession? Did they simply stand there? Did they nod? Did they look bewildered? What for instance was the expression on the faces of Thomas and Philip, the one given to doubting, the other so painfully dim-witted? We do not know, but before we write off the decision for the disciples, what to think about Jesus, as simple because he was there among them, put yourselves in their shoes. They had a struggle but Peter took the plunge and showed the way out, the right way. At that moment he achieved stature.

3 THE SUFFERING MESSIAH

Now the command which Jesus gave to Peter as soon as he had made the great confession 'You are the Christ'. I am quoting from Mark 8.30: 'Then he gave them strict orders not to tell anyone about him.' Why was this? What was he afraid of, should the disciples make public this identification of him as Messiah? It was that he would be hailed as a political Messiah, one who would throw down the enemies of the Jewish people, evict the Roman conquerors of their land, and raise an army, perhaps feed it miraculously as they had seen done with five thousand people. They could go wild with excitement and then what madness would follow, what atrocities, what probable crushing under foot with little hope of recovery.

But Jesus was not that sort of Messiah, not that sort of Christ, and to drive the point home he capped Peter's great confession by telling his disciples gathered there in seclusion at Caesarea Philippi that he 'had to undergo great sufferings, and to be rejected by the elders, chief priests, and doctors of the law; to be put to death, and to rise again three days afterwards'. This was bad news for these twelve men who

76

had hoped that great things lay ahead for them, positions possibly of power and authority in a Messianic State. But the immediate future was not disguised. St Mark says (8.32) 'He spoke about it plainly'. Peter however was not to be put off by this ugly prediction. If Jesus really was the Messiah, and Peter believed it, then death *could not* happen to him, least of all overpowering by his enemies. The Messiah must conquer. So he took hold of Jesus by the arm and began to rebuke him. We find this hard to imagine but St Mark, whose gospel is without frills, has it down in black and white. St Matthew (16.22) tells us what he said: 'Heaven forbid! . . . No, Lord, this shall never happen to you.' What follows bears all the marks of authenticity. 'But Jesus turned round', it was a typical action of his to face those he was addressing 'and' (I am quoting again) looking at his disciples – all of them one by one? – 'rebuked Peter. Away with you, Satan, you think as men think, not as God thinks.' Strong words! Did Jesus at that moment see the tempter behind Peter seeking to divert him from that forthcoming death; the temptation was sharp, horribly sharp, but Jesus, the Messiah, believed that ugly death to be what God thought right for him.

4 OUR TURNING-POINT

We have now come to the turning-point in our estimate of the historical Jesus. Are we satisfied to call him the sublime teacher, the compassionate healer, the strong man whose words and works compel attention, even demanding from us a change of direction in our thinking and living? These estimates are not to be despised. Men and women followed this Jesus. They received his proclamation of the Kingdom of God as true and real, some even saw it embodied in Jesus himself. They believed that if people went his way the world would be a better place. But what about this death by crucifixion? Has this to be taken into our judgement about Jesus? Was it perhaps an accident, could it have been, ought it perhaps to have been, avoided? What is this about a crucified Messiah? The twelve disciples gathered at Caesarea Philippi found this impossibly hard to incorporate into their thinking about their admirable Master. But he had left Galilee especially to bring them to this secluded place in order to ask them the great question and to receive Peter's great answer. There was nothing casual or accidental about it. The time had come, the turning-point had been reached. Galilee with all its wonder and attraction was left behind. Now they would be proceeding into Judaea and see at the top of an ugly little hill a cross, instrument of purposeful cruelty.

16

HIS FACE CHANGED

And while he was praying the appearance of his face changed and his clothes became dazzling white.

LUKE 9.29 (NEB)

On 6 August the Church celebrates the transfiguration of Jesus. And immediately . . . you stop listening, if indeed you have even started to listen. Transfiguration is not a word most of use. We don't hear it in the supermarket. The man or woman in the bus queue is not likely to be overheard talking about transfiguration. Nevertheless the transfiguration of Jesus was one of the five *major* events in his life, three of which we know—his birth (Christmas), his death (Good Friday), his resurrection (Easter Day). But what about the other two? One is his baptism in the River Jordan when he was empowered by the Holy Spirit for his work and the other is his transfiguration which we commemorate on 6 August. What happened? What does transfiguration mean? What has it to do with us?

1 ENCOURAGEMENT

Let me try and tell you in a few words. Jesus was under pressure, terrible pressure. His enemies were closing in and he knew it. I can't say if he had ever seen a crucifixion, but they weren't all that rare. The Romans used crucifixion as a deterrent against rebellion which being the case the victims were not draped over or hushed up. Unless Jesus altered his message and capitulated, crucifixion is what loomed up at the end of the road for him. But he could not talk about it. His disciples would not understand. They thought in terms of political triumph, not sacrificial death. So Jesus was horribly alone. And then it happened. Taking three of his closest disciples, he climbed a nearby mountain and there in the loneliness before their eyes, he was transfigured. They were astonished, indeed more than a little frightened. They scarcely recognized him. He looked

78

so different. His face was different. Instead of the Galilean man in the drab dress of the ordinary local he *shone* like some celestial figure. Indeed heaven clearly owned him, for they heard a voice saying 'This is my beloved Son'. Then the vision—if it was a vision—as suddenly vanished and the same Jesus was with the three disciples as before. Then they descended the mountain. That was the transfiguration. Are we surprised that the disciples did not talk about it? They were too overawed.

Now there are those who will explain this in psychical terms. I am not qualified for this. I cannot claim to be a mystic or anything approaching a mystic. My Christian commitment is a simple thing based on faith and reason, reason and faith. And what I see first of all in this incident is God's infinite mercy in encouraging his faithful servant Jesus in the awesome ministry that faced him in the very near future absolutely alone.

Perhaps you think he didn't need encouragement! But he was a human being like you and me set in a world that can sometimes turn nasty. And who is there wholly ignorant of how this feels? Here is a man who has lost his job. Here is a workman whose employer has turned against him. Here is a woman who has lost her baby. Here is a boy who has failed his examinations. Here is a businessman who has invested his money in a fraudulent firm. I could go on. So could you. And suppose you are alone with no one with whom you can share your fear. I tell you, I tell you fortunate is the man or woman who at such a time believes in a God who provides for us unexpected encouragement when we are down in the drains of apprehension. God sustains his servants who trust him. We are not alone. Let this transfiguration give to us first of all a message of reassurance. God knows and God cares whatever are the rough patches of life we are sometimes called to cross. So be strong and of good courage.

2 EXPERIENCES OF AWE

And now something else from this transfiguration scene. We need experiences of awe, wonder and grandeur in the course of our lives. If we believe the gospel we must believe that at the end of our earthly pilgrimage is glory. Very well then, we need from time to time *anticipations* of that glory. We cannot continue with a perpetual routine of ordinariness.

I think I have told this story before, but I tell it again. Some years ago I was sitting on the deck of a steamer on Lake Thun in Switzerland journeying from Interlaken to Spiez. All the passengers, including myself, sitting side by side were not a little glum. It was supposed to be a beautiful evening and we were there expecting to revel in the panoramic beauty all around us, but instead nothing but murky cloud-cover, wrapping up everything in a depressing greyness. All of a sudden a Frenchman jumped up and pointing with outstretched arm and hand cried out at the top of his voice, 'Regardez, regardez'. And we did, all dozens and dozens of us, we looked where he was pointing; and there in a sudden break in the clouds was the complete Jungfrau, its snow cap gleaming with a dazzling whiteness tinged with pink evening sunlight against a patch of azure sky. It was a transfiguration, and it took our breath away. Our steamer chugged on and the murky mist descended but we had had our vision of glory and covered the rest of the journey with near contentment.

Shall I be suggesting too much if I make the point that this is what our worship in church should do for us—provide us with a flash of eternal glory? I am not pleading for excessive ritual and over-elaborate music but I *am* pointing a critical finger at the sheer ordinariness of too much of our contemporary parochial worship. Our modern liturgies cannot escape all the blame here nor some of our modern translations of the Bible. We need some grandeur, please. Archbishop Cranmer with his Book of Common Prayer was surely right in this; and in this respect at least the Authorized Version of the Bible has not been surpassed. But whatever version is read let it be read with sensitivity to the Transcendent which to some extent it is uncovering. We need some grandeur, please. And I have a strong feeling that people are looking for this in worship, if they are to worship at all, which is partly why cathedral services at the present time are well attended. In some ways this is the age of the cathedral; their services can meet a real need.

Yes, we are in a cathedral.* I live in a village. Let this festival of the Transfiguration remind us that all worship, however humble, is there to part the clouds of life a little bit so that we may catch a glimpse of eternal glory providing another dimension to life's plainness and may be drabness. We are destined for eternity and God has not forgotten us.

* Canterbury Cathedral

3 A DIFFERENT VIEW OF THE HISTORICAL JESUS

One last point. Jesus was transfigured on that mountain top in Galilee and three disciples saw him differently. He was in their eyes no longer just the superb Teacher, the astonishing healer of people's physical and sometimes tormented minds, no longer the strong courageous leader, he was the incarnate Son of God utterly beyond compare, an awesome figure.

I do not think we have begun to see Jesus aright until we have glimpsed (I put it no stronger), until we have glimpsed this other dimension. He it is to whom at the end of each day we can but bow the head and worship—'My Lord and my God'. Jesus needs to be transfigured for us, changed from being an impressive figure in history, into a contemporary Divine presence we can trust. It is the function of worship to make this transference in word and in sacrament, in liturgy and in music, yes even in architecture. God grant us the experience of *worship with glory* in our day and generation.

17

FACING THE END

As the time approached when he was to be taken up to heaven, he set his face resolutely towards Jerusalem, and sent messengers ahead.

LUKE 9.51 (NEB)

I invite you now to consider the second part of the ministry of Jesus now that he no longer worked in Galilee with Capernaum as his centre, but left it all behind. Henceforth there was no centre but a slow journey, possibly over some weeks or even months making for its final destination – Jerusalem. It was a different Jesus that people saw but the same Jesus, a different face but the same face: now its characteristic was determination. It had shone with glory on Mount Hermon, come to be called the Mount of Transfiguration, but that glory had gone when the next morning he made the descent to the valley below. There he met the nine disciples who did not ascend the mountain failing miserably to respond to a father's plea to heal his epileptic son. Apparently they lacked the faith and the power. And there in the crowd were lawyers come all the way from Galilee gloating no doubt over this humiliating failure. Then it was that irritation, if not exasperation, showed up on his face. 'What an unbelieving and perverse generation!' he blurted out, 'How long shall I be with you and endure you all?' And then, peremptorily, 'Bring your son here'. Then, the healing accomplished amid the general wonder and admiration, he addressed his disciples : 'What I now say is for you: ponder my words. The Son of Man is to be given up into the power of men.' But their faces were a blank. And so far off were they from comprehending that they began an argument among themselves as to who was the greatest among them, no doubt with jealous eyes towards Peter, James and John who had been taken up the mountain and witnessed his glory. Would these three be given chief seats in the coming Kingdom? Shame!

1 ST LUKE FILLS IN THE STORY

I have to ask you to bear with me for a minute or two while I say something about the narratives in the gospels on which we are dependent as we try to piece together the story at this point. St Mark's gospel was written first. When St Matthew and St Luke came to write their gospels they used St Mark's gospel as a basis and in general followed his outline but they also seem to have had access to another source of information and incorporated material from it. As well as this they each had knowledge of events and sayings of Jesus independently of these two sources and incorporated them into their gospels. This understanding of the literary background of the first three gospels helps to explain the curious combination of resemblances and differences between them. The fourth gospel, of course, was written somewhat later than the other three and stands by itself. I am drawing your attention to these literary questions now because the part of the story of Jesus to which we are about to give our attention draws very largely on St Luke's gospel. Evidently he had a source of information all his own telling many things Jesus said and did on that journey to Jerusalem of which St Mark and St Luke seem to have known very little. To set out exactly the order and location of the events however is not possible. St Luke's aim was not to provide an itinerary but stories helping us to see more of Jesus than we otherwise would. Some of the stories and parables are the best known, for example the Good Samaritan and the Prodigal Son. These were given on that long journey up to Jerusalem with his face resolutely set. What happened on the way was overshadowed by what was to come at the end.

Let me give illustrations.

When they set out Jesus and his disciples proceeded to pass through Samaria. It was the direct route but Jews frequently avoided it because of Samaritan hostility. They ran into this at once. Some villagers blocked his path because he was on the way to Jerusalem counting this as an insult to their temple on Mount Gerizim, whereupon James and John, two fiery disciples, asked leave of Jesus to call down fire from heaven on them. They reckoned a show of force was the only way to deal with opponents. They earned a stern rebuke from Jesus. It was not his way. This was a bad start to the journey.

Further on, a man was so impressed by Jesus that he offered to become a disciple. 'I will follow you wherever you go' he said, only to receive a forthright dismissal of his burst of sudden enthusiasm for the little it was worth: 'Foxes have their holes, the birds their roosts; but the Son of Man has nowhere to lay his head', from which we are to gather not that Jesus was some kind of vagrant but that his ministry at this stage had no kind of permanent base; he was always on the move. Discipleship therefore at this stage would involve the sacrifice of life's normal pleasures and responsibilities. Similarly when Jesus himself called a man to follow him, he asked for some delay until his father was dead and he was free of family ties. He was put off without more ado. 'Leave the dead to bury their dead; you must go and announce the kingdom of God.' Jesus' ministry was coming to an end, there was no time to lose.

2 THE SOCIAL JESUS

The journey to Jerusalem was not rough all the way, there were occasions of social hospitality some warm, some awkward. Outstanding was the welcome where a woman named Martha welcomed Jesus into her home, possibly on the occasion of a diversionary visit to Jerusalem for a festival, for her village was nearby. We have to ask why she gave this invitation. She wasn't ill, nor was she concerned about someone else in trouble. It could only be that she invited him *for his sake alone*. Woman-like she sensed his weariness and woman-like she offered the rest and refreshment of her home. She cared about him. She cared for him. And guessing how poorly he must often be fed she determined to provide him with a splendid meal prepared by herself. So as soon as he was settled in the comfort of her house, probably well-to-do, she busied herself in the kitchen, but Jesus was not left alone. She had a sister called Mary who was only too willing to sit quietly and listen to all he had to say. Peace reigned in that home that day even though there was a slight ruffle when Martha complained that Mary was not helping in the kitchen, which ruffle Jesus quietly soothed. Much time is too often wasted in trying to estimate which was the better of these two woman: they were both good in their different ways; far more important is to see how human was the historical Jesus. He responded to the natural caring of women. He was not aloof. He welcomed what they especially had to give. And note this. He was completely unlike some religious leaders who feel their leadership requires them always to be the givers of benefits. Jesus was willing to receive, and to receive from two women, possibly well-to-do.

But there was a different kind of social occasion indeed more than one. Luke 11.37 reads 'When he had finished speaking, a Pharisee invited him to a meal'. We prick up our ears. A *Pharisee* invited him to dinner! But were not the Pharisees hostile to him? Yes, indeed, but this one, this day, must have been fascinated by what Jesus had been saying. Even Pharisees had to admit that he was a compelling speaker, whether in a pulpit or in conversation at a dinner table. But this dinner got off to a bad start. The host was put off because his guest, after he had sat down, had not 'begun by washing before the meal'. This has nothing to do with personal hygiene, nothing to do with dodging the cloakroom as if Jesus were ignorant of civilized behaviour. The omission referred to the veritable palaver —no other word will do—about the elaborate *ceremonial* washing which went on at table before the meal was even allowed to begin. Jesus read his host's thoughts. 'You Pharisees!', he said. 'You clean the outside of cup and plate; but inside you there is nothing but greed and wickedness. You fools! Did not he who made the outside make the inside too? But let what is in the cup be given in charity, and all is clean . . .'

I used to worry about this line of denunciatory language on the part of Jesus till I read a collection of the thoughts and sermons of Johann Christopher Blumhart entitled *Vom Glauben bis ans Ende* (1945). Now I see that these denunciations were uttered with a sigh and probably a kind of pitying smile: 'Oh you Pharisees, you clean the outside of cup and plate . . .', saying in effect, 'how silly you are!' All the same it would not have been an easy meal, but Jesus did not allow himself to be diminished by the hospitality; hospitality can be used as an instrument for this, he took the lead, he dominated the scene. He was like that. He was always in command of the situation in which he found himself. Yet he was accessible to all. There is no record of him turning down an invitation whether it came from the very rich or the very poor, the sick or the healthy in body and soul or both, men or women, insiders or outsiders. And this openness to people was in no way curtailed though he was on the road to Jerusalem to die.

18

HARD SAYINGS

On leaving those parts he came into the regions of Judaea and Transjordan; and when a crowd gathered round him once again, he followed his usual practice and taught them.

MARK 10.1 (NEB)

A few years ago I spent Holy Week away responding to an invitation to give a series of addresses on the crucifixion. One free morning I realized that I was only some twenty miles distant from the scenes of my adolescent years where and when the Christian faith became real for me as a result of which I am in the ministry today. So I caught a local train and walked about the streets in the cold sunshine, stood looking at my old school, the church where I sang in the choir, and the house where my family had lived. I suppose I enjoyed the visit. I am not sure. It brought back a mixture of memories sharpening the awareness that I did not belong there any more in any way.

What I am describing is not unusual. Most people are moved by the recollection of the early scenes of their lives. They like to revisit them. I think Jesus must have known this experience. This is partly why on that long last journey up to Jerusalem to face the end of his life soon to come he turned aside to spend time in the regions of Judaea and Transjordan. It was there that the call of God to his ministry had come to him in an unforgettable fashion and he was empowered by the Spirit of God to carry it out. What a crowded tumultuous time had followed! What struggles with and on behalf of people! What pressure from the crowds! What oppositions! What consolations! And now, what lay ahead? Was he not acutely aware that he was in Judaea and Transjordan *as an escapee* from the most recent attempt of his enemies to seize him?

The stay in those parts however was no time for melancholy and brooding inactivity. He was not like that. My text from Mark 10.1 summarizes the situation. 'On leaving those parts he came into the regions of Judaea and Transjordan; and when a crowd gathered round him once again, he followed his usual practice and taught them.'

1 MARRIAGE AND DIVORCE

The teaching was forced out of him on this occasion as a consequence of an attack by some Pharisees. They had followed him
there and had no intention of letting him escape. They had a loaded
question ready with which they felt confident he could be netted.
It sounded innocent enough. 'Is it lawful for a man to put away his
wife?' They knew the law of course as set out in Deuteronomy
24:

> When a man taketh a wife, and marrieth her, then it shall
> be, if she find no favour in his eyes, because he hath found
> some unseemly thing in her, that he shall write her a bill of
> divorcement, and give it in her hand, and send her out of his
> house.

They asked the question not for information but because they
judged he would either side-step this law or repudiate it, then
they would charge him with being a lawbreaker. But he fulfilled
neither of their expectations. He asked them what the law was,
and when they recited it, agreed that it was so. This must have
shaken them. He had however more to say. 'It was because you were
so unteachable that he made this rule for you.' Then he lifted the
whole matter on to a higher level, that is to say to *the principle
of marriage* as God sees it;

> but in the beginning, at the creation, God made them male and
> female. For this reason a man shall leave his father and mother,
> and be made one with his wife; and the two shall become one
> flesh. It follows that they are no longer two individuals, they
> are one flesh. What God has joined together, man must not
> separate.

The disciples, overhearing this stricture against breaking up a
marriage, found the standard of marriage implied too lofty to accept,
and for many people since, this is also true. Whatever the difficulties, however, and they do exist, what must not be denied is
that permanence of the marriage bond is *what Jesus taught*. The
Church must proclaim this because he taught it, and many of
her members, and others outside the Church do keep to it recog-
nizing its wisdom. There will nevertheless be failures and they
must be viewed with charity. What must not be denied is that
they are failures. They are declensions from the teaching of the
historical Jesus.

87

2 CHILDREN AND THE KINGDOM OF GOD

There was an immediate sequel to this *contretemps* about divorce. The disciples wished to pursue with Jesus their own doubts about the high standard of marriage he advocated. They did so away from the crowds in a house. Presumably looking out through the open door they saw women queuing up bringing their children for him to touch. Clearly the women's estimate of Jesus was that simply his touch would be beneficial. This is how they saw 'the Great Rabbi', as they probably called him. They did not expect to be repudiated. They did not expect qualifications to be necessary before he would accede to their request either religious, educational or social. This was not however how the disciples read the situation. They saw the women as intruders to be ejected, intruders upon the important conversation they were having with Jesus about divorce. No doubt they also thought it unbecoming for their revered teacher to be cluttered up with mothers and babies. So they scolded the women. Their action was a window on how they saw Jesus. But they had blundered, blundered badly. Jesus was not often angry but he was on this occasion, he was indignant with his disciples. 'Let the children come to me', he said, 'do not try to stop them; for the kingdom of God belongs to such as these. I tell you, whoever does not accept the kingdom of God like a child will never enter it.' And then they saw what they never forgot. They saw him not simply acceding to the mothers' requests to touch their babies, but actually put his arms round them, and not only that but lay his hands on them and bless them. What? The naughty ones, the good ones, the clean ones and the dirty ones? But they were children. That was enough, and they had been brought to him, that too was enough. The disciples still had a great deal to learn about their Master, but they learnt something that day. It is unlikely that they tried to turn anyone away from him again.

3 PRIVATE PROPERTY

The hard sayings of Jesus about marriage and divorce were followed by hard sayings about private property. It happened like this.

As he was starting out on a journey presumably another stage on the long road to Jerusalem, a stranger came running up to him, young, well-dressed and obviously affluent. He knelt to Jesus, which in itself said much before even a word was spoken. Then he put

88

his surprising question: 'Good Master' (Greek *didaskale agathe*, Good Teacher), 'what must I do to win eternal life?', surprising because on the lips of a young landed proprietor, which is what the words used here for 'great wealth' mean. Evidently all he possessed failed to give him inner satisfaction, an experience not unknown for rich men before or since. In reply Jesus first of all checked his easy facility in labelling him 'good'. Not that he wasn't good but his was a goodness being developed the hard way through life's experience. God alone is absolute goodness. Poor rich young man! Did he grasp this subtle thinking? It is doubtful, but Jesus came at once to practicalities. 'You know the commandments?' Of course he did. No short cuts then, behaviour counts in the matter of eternal life, behaviour towards our fellow human beings. So, Jesus began his enumeration of the ten commandments with number five, omitting numbers one to four dealing with our duty to God, and also changing the order, which in itself is intriguing. Then another surprise. 'But, Master, I have kept all these commandments since I was a boy.' Jesus looked straight at him. Three times over in this story we are told about that look of Jesus. Then this: 'his heart warmed to him' (RV 'loved him'), a rare expression but used also of his attitude to the apostle John. Truly this was a remarkable interview; not least the words which follow: 'One thing *you* lack' (and anyone reading this Scripture in public must place the emphasis on *you*), 'One thing *you* lack: go, sell everything you have, and give to the poor, and you will have riches in heaven; and come, follow me.' Evidently then this young man had more than this one thing to do to win eternal life, he had also to follow Jesus. This was too much, his face registered his struggle, 'he went away with a heavy heart'; not running in the way he had come, we may be sure. And Jesus let him go. He was like that.

Then he 'looked round at his disciples'. O those eyes of his! Who would ever forget that characteristic looking? 'How hard it will be for the wealthy to enter the kingdom of God!' he said. The disciples were taken aback, but he went on 'It is easier for a camel to pass through the eye of a needle than for a rich man to enter the Kingdom of God'. The disciples were more astonished than ever for they read this in terms of utter impossibility. 'Then who can be saved?' They had a point. Rich men need not be absorbed in the daily scramble for daily bread, they have time, if they wish, to give to matters of the Spirit. Again Jesus looked them in the face. 'For man it *is* impossible', he said, 'but not for God; to God everything is possible.'

So riches do not necessarily block all rich people off from the Kingdom of God, everything is possible to God, everything depends on whether those possessed of riches are willing to ground their ultimate security for time and eternity in God and not in their own achievement or bank balance. Riches are not in themselves bad. Everything depends on how they were acquired and what use is made of them. There have to be riches. The world cannot operate without them. The poor and maimed in life cannot be assisted without them. What is required is that those who possess money shall not use it only for themselves but for others. Following Jesus requires this and following Jesus is the way to the Kingdom of God and this is eternal life.

The story isn't finished. It has an unexpected sequel. If the possession of riches may be spiritually risky so is the voluntary sacrifice of them. Peter got caught here, caught in the net of spiritual pride! He watched the rich young man go away with a heavy heart because he could not bring himself to part with his wealth. Peter decided how much better he and all the disciples were than he. 'We here', he said, 'have left everything to become your followers.' Did he puff out his chest? Jesus promised that they would be rewarded but not simply in the way they expected. 'Many who are first will be last and the last first.' God's pecking order is very surprising.

If we follow Jesus along the road up to Jerusalem, his last journey, we shall have to hear the hard sayings.

19

THE DIVINE INTRUDER

*And remember, if the householder had known what time the burglar
was coming he would not have let his house be broken into. Hold
yourselves ready, then, because the Son of Man will come at the
time you least expect him.*

LUKE 12.39, 40 (NEB)

What a strange text! More strange still when you note that these
are the words of Jesus here called the Son of Man. He says that
he operates like a burglar. Hear the words again: 'And remember,
if the householder had known what time the burglar was coming
he would not have let his house be broken into. Hold yourselves,
ready, then, because the Son of Man will come at the time you least
expect him.' I know about burglars, and not surprisingly. My wife
and I have suffered a total of six break-ins to our home, not here
but when we lived in London; although the house was barred and
bolted like a prison. Every house in the little street where we were
for nearly twenty years was burgled several times. We never got
used to it. No one ever does. Even now in the country we can't bring
ourselves to go out into the garden without locking the door behind
us. Burglars sneak up on you. They take you off your guard. They
certainly do not announce when they are coming. And here is Jesus
telling us that he comes like a burglar. What are we to make of it?

1 THE HISTORICAL JESUS AS A BURGLAR

First I ask you to notice that Jesus broke into history like a burglar.
That is to say, he came quietly, unobtrusively, there was no fanfare
of trumpets, no red carpet, no delegations from public bodies to
meet him. He wore no royal robes, carried no sceptre. Of course
this need not worry us in the slightest if he was simply an ordinary
man, or even an extraordinary man; this is how almost everyone
of us comes into the world. But suppose, just suppose the Church
is right in counting him as the Messiah, the Christ, the Son of God,

91

God incarnate, come to save mankind, then how strange that he should come so silently. But he did. Quite suddenly the people of Galilee and the regions round about were aware of an authoritative preacher in their midst and a healer of diseases, even the most obstinate, a man who apparently could cure blindness and restore living power to atrophied limbs. And he did not disclose his identity, at least not more than that he had been a carpenter in Nazareth. His clothes told people nothing, he was dressed like everyone else. His advent into the stream of life in Palestine was unexpected like that of a burglar. And there were those who became bent on getting rid of him. These were the religious and political leaders. They reckoned he was stealing their influence with the people. None could preach as he, heal sufferers as he. He was a disturbing influence, a disturber of the *status quo*, a critic of tradition, and his arguments were dangerously convincing. He must be put out and if that meant death, so be it. They wished to evict the burglar.

Is there a lesson for us here? I think there is. We cannot tell where and when God will become real to us. We cannot plan it. We cannot prevent it. It will simply happen and the advice to us is that we should be ready for it when it does happen. This is the advent message, or in the words of Jesus himself, 'Hold yourselves ready, then, because the Son of Man will come at the time you least expect him', in short, just like a burglar.

2 DIVINE INTRUSION IN OUR EXPERIENCE

Do I need to spell this out? Have you not undergone the experience of attending church service after church service and finding it boring? You wonder why you go on with attending. And then, one Sunday, or maybe not a Sunday, to use a rough and ready expression, 'the whole thing comes alive', in a strange way you are suddenly aware of God. It is impossible to predict or plan when this may take place. The occasion might be an evangelistic campaign, it might be sung Eucharist in a cathedral, it might be an oratorio sung by some massed choirs in a concert hall, it might not be a religious place or occasion at all. It could be out in the country on a glorious autumn day with the trees a riot of red and brown colours. In those moments all the modern gods like materialism, secularism, hedonism and agnosticism fade away, suddenly the real God breaks into the consciousness.

There is another kind of occasion altogether when God may steal into our awareness. This is when the smooth tenor of our life is seriously disturbed. We haven't for once got everything under our control. An illness may be one such occasion, a spell in hospital. Suddenly it comes home to us that we are dependent creatures. And then, as it were, we see God at the window. Probably we keep the experience to ourselves. We think no one would understand. And maybe few would, though some might know what is meant when the occasion is not a serious setback but an exhilarating event like an engagement to marry, an actual wedding, especially if it seems almost too good to be true, and the birth of a child, especially the first child. How is it that parents, relations and friends arrive at church for the baptism, quite often people who may otherwise rarely be seen there? God like a burglar is stealing into their consciousness though they are scarcely aware of it.

And something else—intrusions into our plans. Here is a man, here is a woman who has set aside a whole day to engage in some charitable work, to clean up the church garden, to decorate some old person's home, to undertake the preparation for the annual sale of work, the proceeds to be given some worthy charity. These jobs take time. And the telephone rings. It is someone in great trouble asking if they could 'come round' for advice. You know that kind of counselling will take the whole morning. What should you do? What does God want you to do? Let me tell you, this is something that happens to the vicar of a parish time and time again. He has his diary all neatly mapped out, or he should have, and then the whole plan is ruined. Or is this God intruding as a burglar? He wants us for a work we have not planned. We had better not resent the intrusion. We had better take it as divine guidance as to what we should do on that day. So the need is to hold ourselves ready because God's guidance often comes at a time when we least expect it, or really want it. Some of us who have had to plan our days with series of appointments tend to be bound by our diaries, we need to note these words of Jesus about the burglar. We must be ready for intrusions into our programme and not resent them.

Will you forgive me if I introduce a theological phrase here? It is the 'Divine Initiative', shorthand for covering the belief that God is the prime mover in the course of events, world events and human affairs. Man does not control everything, even if he thinks he does or it appears as if he does, the initiative is with God. Of course if God is in no way personal, but is simply an intellectual concept, more a kind of *it* than a *he*, that is to say an idol, even if not of wood or stone, then to speak of a divine initiative is nonsense. He is just there, he does nothing, he initiates nothing.

If however we come back to the historical Jesus, if we become convinced that in seeing him we are seeing what God is like, how can we not believe that God is operative in the affairs of men and women and it is for us to recognize his activity? Yes, even though he so often comes as an intruder, comes like a burglar.

3 THE SECOND COMING

And back now to the text taken from the Scripture appointed to be read in Advent: 'Hold yourselves ready, then, because the Son of Man will come at the time you least expect him.'

There came a day towards the close of the ministry of Jesus in Judaea when he was leaving the Temple and one of his disciples, with admiration, drew his attention to the massive architecture and splendour of the place. His reply must have been disconcerting, 'You see these great buildings? Not one stone will be left upon another; all will be thrown down.' And a little later when he was sitting on the Mount of Olives facing the Temple he was questioned privately by Peter, James, John and Andrew, 'Tell us', they said, 'when will this happen?' He went on to speak of battles to come, of nations warring with nations, earthquakes and famines, all of which would be the birth-pangs of the new age. And then the Son of Man will be seen coming in the clouds with great power and glory; but exactly when this will be 'no one knows, not even the angels in heaven, not even the Son; only the Father' . . . 'Keep awake, then; for you do not know when the master of the house is coming.'

This is usually referred to as the Second Coming, brought to our notice chiefly in Advent but announced in the acclamations of the Alternative Service Book, Eucharistic Rite A every Sunday, 'Christ has died, Christ is risen, Christ will come again'. It is not easy to visualize this, I would go so far as to say impossible. Suggestions are made that the phrase 'Christ will come again' should be replaced by 'Christ is Lord of all'. The wording has however withstood criticism not least on the grounds that it enshrines the belief that history will not go on for ever and ever but there will be an end. Jesus will be seen then not as he was at the first advent, the man of Galilee, but triumphant as the King of Glory. That second coming will be unpredictable, a sudden interruption into the course of events, an intrusion, a break-in like that of a burglar, but not to steal but to redeem, remake and transfigure a troubled world. Can we hold fast to this belief in the Second Advent? Even when some

94

religious sects, as recently in Korea, have brought the whole idea into disrepute? I am sure we must because it is firmly rooted in the reported teaching of the historical Jesus.

*   *   *

Let me end on a severely practical note. The call to us is to be alert to the thought that God may break into our lives when we least expect his coming, not only in strictly religious settings, sometimes in bleak periods of life, sometimes in gloriously shining times. God has the initiative. He will come how and when he will. He is an intruder. In that sense he is like a burglar, as Jesus himself said (Luke 12.39–40) but not to steal, not to break up, not to spoil but to remake and to bless. Advent is the call to welcome his coming whenever and wherever it shall be.

20

THE DISFIGURED JESUS

He was despised and rejected by men; a man of sorrows, and acquainted with grief; and as one from whom men hide their faces he was despised, and we esteemed him not.

ISAIAH 53.3 (RV)

We read this every Good Friday and although it comes from the Old Testament, written long before the historical Jesus, we do not question its aptness to describe what I am going to call the disfiguration of Jesus. In a previous sermon I spoke about the *transfiguration* of Jesus, how on a mountain top in the presence of three of his disciples, Peter, James and John, his face was suffused with ineffable glory and even his garments became glistening white, and there came a voice from heaven, 'This is my beloved Son, hear him'. There has been some uncertainty exactly how to understand this transfiguration. Was it an actual event or was it perhaps a vision? Could it be that the gospel writers have antedated what was in fact a post-Easter appearance of the risen Christ? If there is some uncertainty about the transfiguration of Jesus there can be none about the disfiguration. It happened. It is hard brutal fact. On Good Friday (so called) that radiant figure was mutilated so that he became 'as one from whom men hide their face'. There was nothing to admire in that twisted, contorted wreck of a human being nailed up to a stake stuck in the ground. Why then has this vandalized, this disfigured Jesus, been displayed in paintings, stained glass, and sculpture in thousands upon thousands of churches all over the world? Why not representations of Jesus in the full radiance of his attractive manhood? Why not Jesus laying on his hands to heal the sick? Why not Jesus stilling the storm? Why not Jesus preaching powerfully in the Galilean synagogues? Why not Jesus rebutting the verbal attacks of the religious authorities of his day? Instead the centre of the stage is given to a Jesus made repulsive by what was done to him on Good Friday, so horrible it is toned down, not least by that loincloth unrealistically imposed to cover his stark nakedness.

1 THE HISTORICAL JESUS BYPASSED

Now of course you Christian people in the congregation will not be slow to come up with an answer, perhaps phrased in the words of this same Isaiah chapter 53 from which I took my text, and you would not be wrong.

> Surely he has borne our griefs and carried our sorrows; yet we esteemed him stricken, smitten by God, and afflicted. But he was wounded for our transgressions, he was bruised for our iniquities; and the chastisement of our peace was upon him; and with his stripes we are healed.

We make the cross of Christ central, we display the crucifix because that is the price Jesus was willing to pay for our rescue from self destroying self-centredness. We must never forget it. We ground our acceptance with God not in what we have done or have not done but in what Christ did *for us* culminating in that horrible crucifixion. All this is true, gloriously true. There can however be an unfortunate consequence of the grateful concentration on the cross and our sinfulness. It is that the *historical Jesus* is passed by, becoming a vague shadowy figure, largely unknown, largely unappreciated. Over against this I thought right to preach this series of sermons on the historical Jesus, so that we could see him as he was, see (so to speak) his face.

One other, and perhaps unexpected, outcome of the Church's concentration on benefits which flow to us from the cross of Christ to the neglect in part of the life of Jesus is that the world *outside the Church* has stepped in with a vibrant interest in it not least during the last two or three decades. The man Jesus of Nazareth has been the subject of popular books, films, plays and even musicals receiving wide publicity; historically inaccurate no doubt, but registering the undying fascination of the subject for people in general. In these portrayals Jesus is seen without the eyes of Christian faith. Some would assert that these portrayals show us the real Jesus, Jesus as he actually was, Jesus without the distorting overloading of Christian dogma, Jesus before he was turned into the theological Christ worked up by such subtle theologies as St Paul's dogmatisms, for example, the Crucifixion as the atonement. And so a recent book bore the title *Jesus Before Christ*. This is supposed to be Christianity simplified, Christianity without theology, Christianity as the remarkable (if you like) teaching of an impressive man. So 'the Sermon on the Mount', so called, becomes the central point of Christianity, not the crucified victim on that repulsive little mount at Calvary. Thus Jesus can take his place in our minds in the long line of great teachers of the past who have contributed so much to the well-being of mankind. This is secular man's Jesus.

2 TWO QUESTIONS

In the face of all this I would like to pose two questions. First, is it possible to appreciate Jesus as he really was without Christian faith? And secondly, is there a gospel in this secular presentation of Jesus, Jesus as simply a great figure of history?

First then, is it possible to appreciate Jesus without Christian faith? The answer is 'Up to a point, yes, certainly', but we are left with so many questions. The historical Jesus was, in his time, an enigma, a puzzle, a mystery. The congregation in the Nazareth synagogue where his humble origins were known murmured as they listened to his striking preaching 'Where does he get it all from?' And when the storm on the lake was stilled at his word (if it was) his disciples said to themselves 'Who then is this, that even the winds and the sea obey him?' And the religious authorities complained 'Who is this that can forgive sins?' The fact is, Jesus was so extraordinary in his person that the usual categories of assessment appeared totally inadequate. Some called him a prophet but what sort of a prophet no one could say. Others played with the idea of Messiah but he looked so commonplace in his peasant's garb. The truth seems to be there is an unbridgeable gap between Jesus and our understanding of him *unless* we are willing to leap across it with the Christian faith that he was the Christ, the Anointed One, the Son of God most High. And this leap of faith is most often taken *prior* to any serious study of the historical Jesus. Somehow this faith gets caught in the Christian community or from our family upbringing or from some man or woman we deeply admire, maybe even a mixture of all three. So there comes to be belief in Jesus and out of this belief something like an understanding of Jesus arises, elementary no doubt at first, but this is the important fact. Who Jesus was/is, is known in the first place existentially, that is to say by means of personal experience, not in the first place by a process of reasoning or study. This may come later but in default of initial belief we are left with a yawning gap.

And now the second question. Is there a gospel, is there good news, in the secular view of Jesus? Granted it does not lack admiration for Jesus but it is centred chiefly if not wholly on his teaching, the beatitudes, the parables and the striking metaphors. And they are indeed treasures of wisdom and spirituality but there is scarcely a sentence in them which could not be paralleled in the writings of one or more of the great Jewish Rabbis. And they are superb for the few who have the insight to perceive their meaning, or the willpower to put them into practice, but for the great mass of the community they are way out beyond them as they were for the multitudes who listened to Jesus' teaching in Galilee. Men and women do not only need to be told how they ought to live but also to be given the power to do so. First they need lifting up out of the slough of despond and made alive with hope. They need to know that God cares for them. This good news, this gospel was demonstrated in the wonderful works of Jesus, the healings and restoration of powers to those who had lost or forfeited them; and supremely in that he gave his life.

What all this means is that the person of Jesus is the central issue, Who was he? The answer we give to this question makes all the world of difference to how we see that mutilated, that vandalized figure impaled on a wooden stake outside Jerusalem, terrible to behold, the disfigured Jesus. If it really was for us then there is a gospel to proclaim.

3 WORD AND SACRAMENT

And now let me remind you that it is the disfigured not the transfigured Jesus who is at the centre of our Holy Communion with God. Bread is taken, *broken*, and given to us with the words 'This is my body which is given for you'. Wine is taken, poured out and given to us with the words 'This is my blood which was shed for you'. And all in memory of that night and that last supper with Jesus and his twelve disciples and from which the traitor Judas went out to sell his Master to the men who disfigured him. This partaking of the broken bread and poured-out wine is what the historical Jesus ordained should be in memory of him. His wonderful teaching is not at the centre, nor his astonishing works of healing, that place is occupied by a cross on which he was disfigured and tortured to death. It is there supremely that we communicate with the living God. Did the disciples at the time *understand* the significance of their partaking of the bread and wine at the last supper? How many of us understand it now? But here we are at the point when understanding does not count, nor any other qualification, only that we are willing to *receive*.

When we grasp this centrality of communion with the crucified

Christ we are able to see the history of Jesus, his teaching and his wonderful works in the proper perspective. We shall meditate upon them because they tell of the God with whom we have communion and whom the historical Jesus reveals. There will be a sensitivity to them, and out of that sensitivity a growing measure of understanding.

And so I end with a plea for a proper balance of the altar and the pulpit in Church worship. Sometimes the pulpit has been underrated, sometimes the sacrament of Holy Communion has been underrated. The full ministry is the ministry of Word and Sacrament, and central to both is the disfigured Jesus.

21

THE SECRET OF JESUS' LIFE

Then he (Jesus) *went forward a little, threw himself on the ground, and prayed that, if it were possible, this hour might pass him by. 'Abba, Father', he said, 'all things are possible to thee; take this cup away from me. Yet not what I will, but what thou wilt.'*

MARK 14.35, 36 (NEB)

In January 1993 I had my attention caught, as the attention of thousands and thousands of other people must have been caught, by a striking picture in the newspapers of the actress Audrey Hepburn who died that month. Most of us remember her from the famous film of *My Fair Lady*. She was exceedingly beautiful and very accomplished. Her obituary notice in at least one quality newspaper occupied almost a whole page. But why towards the end of her career did she throw it all up so as to work with UNICEF and devote herself to the welfare of starving and undernourished children? There was another picture in the newspaper showing her with an emaciated little black child in her arms. The answer is that her own adolescence was passed in Holland during the German occupation where she herself experienced hunger and debilitating weakness. At times there were only turnips and tulip bulbs to eat. It was that terrible memory that made her what she was.

Sometimes we ask the question of an unusual man or woman who attracts our attention: What was it, what is it, that makes him or her tick? I hesitate to apply this rough and ready phrase to the historical Jesus but something like it must have been asked a hundred times and more about him. He was so unusual, so attractive, so accomplished, so strong, yet so sensitive to situations and feelings of others, and willing to face suffering himself. What was the secret of his distinctive life and bearing? This is the enquiry I have in mind in today's sermon. You must remember the resurrection had not yet taken place. He was not known as the Christ.

101

1 THE FATHER IN A JEWISH FAMILY

Now I must emphasize at the outset that it is not possible to conduct any sort of psychological analysis of Jesus. We cannot penetrate to his inner mind and feeling. He did not speak about himself. We are limited to the records of his words and actions as set down in the gospels and the impression he made on different people. From these however it is clear that what dominated his whole life was his constant awareness of God as his Father. The phrase 'My Father' occurs seventeen times in St Matthew's gospel, four in St Luke and 25 in St John not counting the parallel passages. The first recorded words of his at the age of twelve according to St Luke are 'Did you not know that I was bound to be in my Father's house?' and his last recorded words also in St Luke's gospel are 'Father, into thy hands I commend my spirit'. It is true to say that from beginning to end his whole life was dominated by the consciousness of God who to him was 'my Father', and for whom he had a special word, namely 'Abba'. This was the secret of the way he lived and what he did.

In order to appreciate this application of the word 'Father' to God we have to bear in mind the normal Jewish life in which he grew up and to which he remained faithful. It was a patriarchal society. The father was the head of the family and the dominant figure. He was authoritative and what he willed was carried out. There was no contending about this in the family. He was also the teacher in the family, the authoritative teacher. More than that he was the provider for the family, he housed them and protected them. And when he died all that he possessed automatically went to his sons. So the words of the father in Jesus' parable of the Prodigal Son to the elder boy: 'My boy, you are always with me, and everything I have is yours.' And then 'How could we help celebrating this happy day? Your brother here was dead and has come back to life, was lost and is found.' Perhaps there is no better picture of the Jewish father in the home as Jesus knew it, not repressive, not without merriment and most noticeable of all, no curtailing of freedom: the younger son was allowed to go off into the far country, although his father feared what would happen to him there. This is the picture Jesus supplied of what a proper father should be and a picture of what God is like as Father.

2 JESUS' RELATIONSHIP WITH GOD THE FATHER

What then does this tell us about Jesus' relationship to God? First and foremost it was an easy, intimate relationship indicated by his name for God, Abba. Some commentators have suggested 'Daddy' as an equivalent. I doubt this. 'Daddy' belongs too much to the stage of childhood and is not used when a man reaches maturity. Jesus called God 'Abba' throughout his life. God for Jesus then was not primarily the King, nor the Judge nor the Lawgiver. He was his heavenly Father, never remote, always at hand. But all power belongs to God and his will is to be accepted. There is however, no compulsion. It can be refused and rejected and very often is, though not in the case of Jesus; that is his distinction. So his prayer in the garden of Gethsemane (my text for this sermon): 'Then he went forward a little, threw himself on the ground, and prayed that, if it were possible, this hour might pass him by. "Abba, Father", he said, "all things are possible to thee; take this cup away from me. Yet not what I will, but what thou wilt."' This willing acceptance of the will of God the Father has testimony borne to it by John 4.34: 'But Jesus said, "It is meat and drink for me to do the will of him who sent me until I have finished his work"' and John 5.30: '. . . my aim is not my own will, but the will of him who sent me' and 6.38: 'I have come down from heaven, not to do my own will, but the will of him who sent me.' All this should make abundantly clear what was the secret of Jesus' life – freely doing the will of Abba, his ever present heavenly Father close at hand.

And now let me take this a stage further. It was because Jesus was in this intimate relationship with God his Father that he was able to perform his wonderful works, so often simply described as miracles. He was not able to perform these because he was God on earth, God in disguise, God dressed up as a man. He was a real man, with the limitations of a man, but in so close a relationship with God by his own purposeful dedication that the will of God, and power of God, and authority of God was openly manifest in him. This close relationship was sustained by a life of prayer with the result that there was a oneness between himself and God, God and himself, so that where he was God was in all his grace and power. This is why when we look at the historical Jesus we can see what God is like.

One more point: the relationship between Jesus and God was unique. It did not exist because of Jesus' nature but because of his complete and willing dedication to Abba his Father. He therefore never bracketed himself with us in calling God his Father. Talking to his disciples, he said 'When you pray say "Our Father"', never 'When *we* pray say "Our Father"'. His relationship to the Father was unique and perfect, ours is spasmodic and imperfect. So John 20.17 talking of the Ascension reads 'I am now ascending to my Father and your Father'—not, you will notice, 'I am now ascending to our Father'. Jesus had a special, a unique relation to his Father Abba by reason of his complete dedication.

All this no doubt has been a little difficult for us to grasp, but the main point will, I trust be clear. The secret of Jesus' life was his unique relation to God. This is what made him what he was.

3 OUR TRUST IN GOD AS FATHER

Is there then any message for us? I think there is. God is *our Father* in heaven. We can take any concern of ours to him. Nothing is too big for him, nothing too small. Our everyday problems and needs can be laid confidently before him in prayer. But we must approach him with reverence and respect. The prayer he taught his disciples, and us, shows us the way: 'Our Father who art in heaven, *hallowed be thy name.*'

The trouble with so many of us is that we rebel against God when things do not turn out as we expect they should. We even give God up, or leave him out of our reckoning. I was told of this little true story. A young woman was married to a German artist and they lived in Berlin. To her great joy a baby was soon on the way and she was determined that the child should be delivered by a gynaecologist not in Germany but in England. This was arranged. The child was born. The English gynaecologist was present but he mismanaged the severance of the umbilical cord and the baby died. The mother took this very badly. She blamed God and though she had been brought up in a Christian home and been a Sunday school teacher, she severed all links with Church from then onward for the rest of her life. So she rebelled. God had let her down and she would have no more use for him. She would manage her own life in future, and she left instructions that when she died she was to be buried with her child here in England. A sad story.

Let me end by saying this. Jesus called all who followed him in Judaea and Galilee to faith in God as Father. We are called to this faith and out of it will come a power for living. No, we shall not be working miracles like Jesus but we shall be in touch with the spiritual resources that allow us to overcome in 'the changes and chances of this mortal life'. Faith in God's will as being the best for us isn't easy. It involves a struggle. It was all that and more for Jesus. Hear my text again: 'Then he went forward a little, threw himself on the ground, and prayed that, if it were possible, this hour might pass him by. "Abba, Father", he said, "all things are possible to thee; take this cup away from me. Yet not what I will, but what thou wilt."' With that he rejoined his disciples and went through with the Cross and Passion that was to follow, and as he breathed his last he prayed 'Father, into thy hands I commend my spirit'. There was no rebellion. There was trust in God the Father's care till the end. It is to this secret of living that we are called. It is the way to follow him whom we call the Christ.

22

JESUS THE JUDGE

*So they came to Jerusalem, and he went into the temple and began
driving out those who bought and sold in the temple.*

MARK 11.15 (NEB)

We are unaccustomed to think of Jesus like this—striding into the
Temple precincts and driving out the traders who operated there.
'Driving' is a strong word but St John in his gospel, antedating the
incident, colours it by telling of the whip of cords which Jesus made
obviously for use. Seeing it some people no doubt took to their heels
and ran, leaving behind them stalls and goods for sale as well as
money scattered across the floor. Birds and animals, there for
purchase at fancy prices for the temple sacrifices, were let loose, the
whole place in total disarray. This was the work of Jesus in the
Temple. Can we believe it?

Perhaps our instinct is to suppress this lurid picture. But his action
is included in all four gospels, a distinction accorded to very few
actions of his. We cannot therefore omit it without distorting, if not
destroying, the total impression of him which the gospel writers
were at pains to present. Or we may attempt to rationalize it and so
tone it down, asserting that what we see here is Jesus as a social
reformer concerned for the ordinary people in the community being
exploited by this public mart at which the Temple authorities winked
because it profited them and their organization. Partly true as this
interpretation may be, the real significance of this 'cleansing of the
Temple', as it is normally called, lies at a much deeper level. This
was the last public action of Jesus before the crucifixion. In it he
was saying something utterly decisive. He was proclaiming the end
of the Jewish cult of animal sacrifice and all the clutter (and it was
immense) that went with it as the way of approach to the presence
of God and the forgiveness of sins. This drastic action was the
climax of Jesus' *teaching* ministry. Nothing he ever did or said up
to this point in his ministry was more significant than this.

106

1 THE AUTHORITY OF JESUS

And now let me set this action in its context. For the last week of his life Jesus went public in a way he had not before. Hitherto he had avoided, even *suppressed* publicity, that is to say he had commanded those whom he had cured of their ailments to say nothing to anyone, and when he began to disclose to his twelve disciples what would befall him at Jerusalem he strictly charged them to keep the knowledge to themselves. This is why he has been called 'the secret Messiah'. On Palm Sunday however, as we have come to call it, this reticence was cast aside. He agreed, even arranged, to be seen riding triumphantly into Jerusalem, albeit on a humble donkey, receiving the acclamations of the crowd lining the route wild with enthusiasm at this public acknowledgement of his leadership.

But what sort of leader? Could there be any doubt? He strode at once into the Temple courts and drove out those who serviced the kind of worship that was conducted there and that helped substantially to finance it to the chagrin of the pilgrims. Here then was Jesus cleaning up the Temple, evicting its fraud and rapacity. More than that, he was acting as judge at the very heart of the Jewish national life. Not surprisingly the authorities were mad with anger, anger stoked by fear of Jesus' influence with the public. No wonder a strong delegation of chief priests, lawyers and elders sought him out to confront him. 'By what authority are you acting like this. Who gave you authority to act in this way?' So this was the sore point, the authority of Jesus. It had been evident from the very beginning of his ministry when he occupied the pulpit in Capernaum to preach, but now it was being exercised not in rural Galilee but in the most public and sensitive centre of Jewish national life, the Temple at Jerusalem.

The religious authorities did not bring him down with their double-barrelled question. 'I will ask you *one* question', he countered, 'and if you give me an answer, I will tell you by what authority I act. The baptism of John: was it from God, or from men?' And then, peremptorily, 'Answer me!' But no answer was forthcoming. His attackers were caught in their own trap. Which ever way they answered they were in difficulties. So they sidestepped. 'We don't know', they lamely replied. 'Then neither will I tell you by what authority I act.' This was not a 'tit for tat' reply on Jesus' part. The ministries of John and Jesus were interlocked. If one was accepted as divinely commissioned and this was the case with John's ministry, then the other must be accepted too . . .

2 PARABLES OF JUDGEMENT

Then fell parable after parable from Jesus' lips, all delivered in these same crowded Temple courts, and all with one theme – judgement. Not however before the disciples themselves had received a striking visual lesson on this. It was an acted parable about a withered fig tree, an incident which has never ceased to puzzle until it is seen as a parable of judgement. The Jewish nation had failed to bring forth ripe fruits of its own special calling by God. The consequences would be devastating.

The first parable puzzled no one. The chief priests, lawyers and elders recognized it at once. It was an attack upon themselves. They were the wicked husbandmen who sought to kill the heir to the vineyard. For this they would be judged and their vineyard be given to others. They got the message and slinking away, were goaded by it to pursue their hostility to Jesus with even more vigour.

One outcome was a group of Pharisees and men of Herod's party sent to trap Jesus (see Mark 12). They opened up within what was supposed to be disarming flattery and then planted their catch question about taxation, a matter of unfailing public sensitivity. 'Are we or are we not permitted to pay taxes to the Roman Emperor? Shall we pay or not?' They reckoned their trap could not fail. If he said 'Yes' he would be in trouble with the Jews. If he said 'No' he would be in trouble with the Romans. But their trap did fail. 'Fetch me a silver piece', he said. 'Whose head is this and whose inscription?' They supplied the only answer possible, 'Caesar's', but hardly expected his comment: 'Pay Caesar what is due to Caesar and pay God what is due to God.' So they were outwitted. Their barbed question was a flop.

One more attempt at defeating him was made, this time by means of ridicule. The Sadducees, a sect more political than religious, came with a cock and bull story about a woman who had seven husbands, one after another, for they all died. Last of all the woman died. Did someone in the crowd shout 'About time too!'? The crowd would love this. But Jesus was not floored. On the contrary he charged the Sadducees with ignorance. There is no marriage in the resurrection. The question simply does not arise. 'You Sadducees ought to know that.' *Exeunt* Sadducees.

There were however two welcome points of relief in this gloomy day of attack and counterattack. A lawyer listening and impressed by Jesus asked 'Which commandment is first of all?' Jesus gave him the two great commandments – 'love of God and love of neighbour. There is no other commandment, greater than these.' And the lawyer came back with a statement from him which was astonishing. 'Well said, Master, to love God and to love neighbour is *far more than any burnt offerings or sacrifices*.' Had this man then grasped the lesson of Jesus' cleansing act at the Temple? Apparently, for Jesus said 'You are not far from the Kingdom of God'.

The other point of light was vastly different. A poor widow dropping two tiny coins in the collecting box, so tiny the treasurer coming across them would scarcely judge them worth adding to the day's total takings. But Jesus calling his disciples insisted that this widow had given more than all the others, for she had given of her penury but they of their superfluity. This took place close to the Temple market where money was raked in from pilgrims paying for their burnt offerings and sacrifices. The widow's action produced Jesus' judgement on the whole system.

All this took place on the Tuesday of Holy Week. Was there ever a Tuesday more crammed with activity, conflicts and judgement? And I have barely recounted the half of what took place. How could I in one sermon? There was Jesus' prediction of the total destruction of the Temple, there was his forthright condemnation of the Pharisees and lawyers for their hypocrisy delivered for the benefit of the crowds and his own disciples. There were the three unforgettable parables, first the ten girls, five of them shut out from a marriage feast for no other reason than imprudence; then the lazy rascal flung out into the dark because he failed to make use of what had been entrusted to him; and thirdly the banishment of the well-endowed who did nothing to relieve their poor neighbours. Strong meat indeed in this teaching! Nothing soft, nothing sloppy. Tuesday was the day when judgement was proclaimed loudly. It was Jesus' final teaching. Hear how St Matthew winds it up in his gospel (26.1 and 2). 'When Jesus had finished this discourse he said to his disciples, "You know that in two days' time it will be Passover, and the son of Man is to be handed over for crucifixion".' The end of the historical Jesus was at hand.

3 INFIDELITY

In the light of all this the question is bound to arise, was Jesus a faithful Jew then? Was he not renegading on the whole Jewish way of life, tearing it to pieces? No, he was not. Jesus was faithful to the very last. He was born a Jew, brought up a Jew, lived all his life as a Jew and died as a Jew, the words of a Jewish psalm on his lips. His complaint was that the nation as a whole had become unfaithful to its heritage. It had turned the law which should have been a delight into a burden weighing it down with over 613 rules and regulations and when that happens, people, finding it too heavy or even ridiculous, seek ways round it. So casuistry comes in and with casuistry a whole tribe of legal technicians adept at working the system (these were called Scribes in Jesus' day) and with the casuistry, hypocrisy, people appearing to be religious but actually using religion to their own advantage, even to fill their pockets, and as a cover-up for their own infidelities. This sort of Judaism, riddled with holes, was grossly in evidence in high places in Jerusalem, not least the Temple. It accounts for Jesus' anger and why he 'cleansed the Temple' in such a forthright fashion. What lay at the root of all this was a profound misconception which it paid the legalists to perpetuate. It was to interpret the Law, which is at the basis of Jewish life, as a set of grim rules and regulations, whereas it is nothing of the kind. The word commonly used for Torah is law, but it really means *teaching*, showing the way it is best to live and make life happy and successful. Once grasp this and we shall not reckon the Psalmist plain stupid when he sang 'Lord, what love have I unto thy law: all the day long is my study in it' (Psalm 119). Jesus did not break with the teaching. He said 'Do not suppose that I have come to abolish the Law (Torah) and the prophets; I did not come to abolish but to complete'. What he looked for was a higher standard of religious life than that of slavish adherence to a set of religious regulations. So he was ready to heal on the Sabbath day, which the Scribes condemned as illegal. The Jews were right, are right, to see the laws as teaching how it is wise to live, what to do and what not to do, but wrong when they make it into a tight legal system. It was at that point that the judgement of Jesus came in strong and clear even in Jerusalem, the very centre of the nation's life.

And now maybe we reckon we can sit pretty to all this. We aren't Jews, we're Christians, and all this that we have been hearing from you Mr Preacher is ancient history. We aren't interested! But listen. What Jesus strongly judged was infidelity. Can we escape the charge of this in the community at large today? Doesn't it stalk the stage? Infidelity in marriage, infidelity in business settlements, infidelity in newspaper reporting, infidelity in politics. Don't we ask on all sides 'Who can you trust today?'? Hasn't the phrase 'economical with the truth' been coined to meet a modern situation? I could go on, so could you. What the historical Jesus did was to state clearly that judgement stands at the door when infidelity is let rip. No, not with a thunderbolt from heaven, but with a slow and inexorable deterioration in the quality of life driving out satisfaction and contentment. We dislike this judgement. Perhaps we dislike this Jesus. We would prefer a harmless Jesus, 'meek and mild'. But was he like that? We shall never know unless we have the patience to see the pictures of the historical Jesus which the gospels in the New Testament present for us.

23

THE END OF THE BEGINNING

The beginning of the gospel of Jesus Christ, the Son of God.
MARK 1.1

No one telling the story of any famous figure of the past can possibly omit some account of the death. The dying is a significant part of the living. So with the historical Jesus. It must find a place in the historical picture. And this constitutes a difficulty for this series of sermons. To give his death the space and significance which the gospel narratives accord it would require a series to itself, and something like this I have attempted elsewhere. On the other hand, if it is only presented summarily, the impression would be left that it is only of marginal significance, and this is clearly contrary to the Christian gospel. What I propose therefore is to devote one sermon, but only one, to the subject in this particular series.

1 DEATH AND DISILLUSIONMENT

Jesus suffered a violent death. There was barely a touch of mercy in it. Certainly none visible from heaven and very little from earth, only the jar of drugged wine set at the foot of the cross by some unknown caring woman (probably) out of sheer pity. Everything else about Jesus' death was brutal and obscene – a naked body pinned with nails in public to a wooden stake stuck in the ground, writhing in gruesome agony, heaving and sagging, oozing with blood and sweat, all control of its natural functions gone, a hideous human exhibit, crawling no doubt with flies. No wonder the gospel writers drew a veil over what actually happened.

The horrible details of this macabre event did not however constitute the real offence of this repulsive death scene but rather that death *in any form* could overtake Jesus. This is what all but drove those who knew him and adored him to unutterable despair. After all what had he done to deserve this? There was no justice in it.

112

And where was God? The crucifixion of Jesus seemed to stand as a public proclamation of the reasonableness of atheism. And what about the observed powers of Jesus in Galilee? Did he really raise from the dead the son of the widow of Nain? Or that daughter of Jairus, the Capernaum synagogue president, lying on a bed, the funeral mourners filling the room? Or Lazarus, brother of Martha and Mary, on the very doorstep of Jerusalem? Did these things happen? Were they faked? Or have 'tall stories' got around? But if the disciples of Jesus actually saw these wonderful works as the gospels say they did, how then could one who possessed such extraordinary powers over the lives and deaths of others fall a victim to death himself? When Jesus attempted to tell his disciples of his forthcoming death as set out in Mark chapters 8, 9 and 10 they simply could not understand and were afraid to ask. All that these men believed or half believed or were coming to believe about the possibility of the man they loved being the Messiah lay in irretrievable ruins. The public dying of Jesus killed all hope for a better world. Apparently evil will always have the last word. It will stalk the earth till the end of time. There is nothing else. Everyone must grow accustomed to meaninglessness from the cradle to the grave. St Luke, ever an artist with words, encapsulated the total deadness resulting from the death of Jesus when he told of two travellers on the Jerusalem to Emmaus road confessing 'But we had been hoping that he was the man to liberate Israel'.

So the story of the historical Jesus ends in the dismal clouds of despair and disillusionment. That radiant personality, those penetrating words of wisdom, the healings brought about by those strong hands, the thrill, the excitement, the sheer power even over matter, added up to nothing unique. All they say is that there lived an extraordinary man, a super-charismatic, of whom stories were told that are hard to believe, but whom death claimed at the end as with everyone else. Let the tale be shut up in the history books. It has nothing much to give us now.

2 RESURRECTION AND HOPE

But the story of the historical Jesus is not shut up in the history books. It is being told over and over again. Millions of people the world over, turn to it with avid attention. And there is a Christian Church strong in some parts of the world, weak in others, surviving at times the most determined opposition, intellectual undermining and ridicule. More than once it has been 'written off' but it lived again and still lives. What is the explanation of all this? It will not be found in the story of the historical Jesus. And it cannot be discovered by a process of reasoning. We have to go outside that story and make a leap of faith. We are driven to it and that only because of the bleakness of the alternatives.

I refer of course to the resurrection of Jesus. If this is true the story of historical Jesus, including the death, is transformed. Death did not claim him at the end. He lived again. Death was beaten. He came to be experienced as the risen Christ. This was good news, pulsating, invigorating good news. There was, there is, a gospel to proclaim and the Church has never ceased to proclaim it. But, and this is the point of importance for this series of sermons on the historical Jesus, the stories about him were treasured and written down because he is the resurrection and the life.

The fourth gospel, St John's gospel, tells the story of Jesus uniquely in the light of the resurrection, which is not to deny that it contains solid historical facts, but it is coloured by a vivid awareness of the risen Christ. Even the account of the crucifixion is presented as a victory over death. It is to St Mark's Gospel that we must turn for the bare history, even the stark story of the crucifixion, telling us what actually happened, and to a large extent St Matthew and St Luke follow this. These are points to remember when the gospel narratives are read telling of the historical Jesus.

3 THE EXTRAORDINARY MEMORIAL

We come back to the death of Jesus. When famous people die and their story is told invariably a memorial is set up, most often at the place of burial. But there is no such memorial for Jesus, nor ever has been. The historical Jesus is not remembered by a tomb but by a cross. It stands as his memorial for ever. This is extraordinary. But we have to face it. The resurrection of Jesus makes it his memorial. It does not do away with the cross, it makes it shine with radiance, the radiance of eternal life. So the story of the historical Jesus is *the beginning* of the gospel of Jesus Christ the Son of God as St Mark expressly labelled it in the opening words of his book—chapter 1 verse 1: 'Here begins the Gospel of Jesus Christ the Son of God' (NEB).

24

THE REVELATION OF GOD

For the same God who said, 'Out of darkness let light shine', has caused his light to shine within us, to give the light of revelation— the revelation of the glory of God in the face of Jesus Christ.

2 CORINTHIANS 4.6 (NEB)

As I cast my mind back over this preaching on the historical Jesus I wonder if I do not hear someone commenting, Yes, Mr Preacher, I have been interested in the story you have been telling about the historical Jesus, as you call him, but I cannot dismiss from my mind the fact that it is history past and gone. We are modern people, we are not interested in history, we are concerned with living today. Of course we need to know the basic facts if we are to pass as, in any sense, educated people. But do we really need to know, for instance, the struggles of those who encountered him, what to think about his identity, who he really was?

And something else. We are Church people. We call Jesus Christ the Lord. We append this title to every prayer we offer. He is not simply an historical figure for us, we celebrate his resurrection, he is for us the risen Christ, the Christ of our experience, become real to us by the Holy Spirit. So we are conscious, intermittently no doubt, nevertheless conscious of Christ as a spiritual presence now especially in the Christian fellowship of the Church otherwise we should not be here. We are not students of history, not even of Christian history. We are men and women struggling to live the Christian life in the contemporary world that is often rough, often sordid and sometimes even hostile. We want strength for living, and peace for dying. To be blunt, Mr Preacher, we don't need this historical background. We can even 'get along' better without it.

1 THREE COUNTER-ARGUMENTS

I recognize the strength of your argument. I even think there is something in it, nevertheless there are three comments I conceive

115

it my duty to make. Firstly, the story of the historical Jesus safeguards and expounds his essential humanity; secondly, it allows us to know the content of the revelation of God he made; thirdly, it provides the qualification for apostleship and indicates where the Church is grounded.

(a) First, then, it safeguards *the humanity of Jesus*. Let me put the matter this way. If we cannot for a while stand away from conceiving of Jesus as Christ and Lord we shall not see him as living the kind of life we have to live, thinking he could always fall back on his divinity. Unlike us, then, he would know what tomorrow would bring forth. Unlike us he would be ignorant of how it feels to be tempted over anything. Unlike us he would never be exasperated, never suddenly angry, never baffled. In which case we shall probably see him as a solemn figure, remote from ordinary life, never laughing, absent from anything like a party, someone always keeping himself to himself, a man to admire maybe, even revered, but not to love, not to adore. You stay away from such a Jesus, he is out of your reach. He cannot come where you and I are.

(b) Now my second comment. We need to study the life of the historical Jesus for *the revelation of God* we find. Not that new truths about him are presented there. What we shall see is truths about God that have always been true but Jesus is the lens through which we mortals are able to discern them. Let me give a homely if inadequate illustration. My house and garden is within about eight miles of Gatwick airport and not surprisingly aircraft are constantly passing overhead within sight, but too high for their nationalities and distant destinations to be read from their markings on the tailpieces and fuselages. And then as a present I was given a pair of binoculars. What a transformation they made for my viewing! The lens made visible what was otherwise almost invisible. Now the historical Jesus is the lens through which we are able to discern what God is like. There are some surprises. God is not an impassive Being distant from the sufferings and turmoil of our world! God suffers with us and because of us. Nor is God one who displays his power and glory, on the contrary he is self-effacing, he even hides himself. Nor is he a sentimental God of love, nor a kind of benevolent grandfather. He may lose patience, be angry, and even become ruthless. Nor has he an indulgent attitude towards the so-called religious, but if anything a predilection for the outsiders. The poor and

116

suppressed are indeed his concern but the rich and successful are not cast aside. All these, and more, are revelations of the nature and character of God which we shall miss unless we are prepared to look through the lens which the historical Jesus makes available for us.

(c) Thirdly, we turn to the Christian Church. It is built upon *the foundation of the twelve apostles*, that is to say they stand for all time as the foundation members. But what qualified them for this exalted position? Their goodness, their devotion, their charitable works? Or was it their witness to the crucifixion and resurrection of Jesus? All of these, but the one essential qualification was to have also been in the close company of the historical Jesus from the time of John's ministry of baptism until the day when he, Jesus, was taken up, the day we call the Ascension. This was made clear when the apostolic number of twelve apostles which Jesus himself had chosen was one short because of the defection of Judas Iscariot who became the traitor. During the period between the Ascension and the coming of the Holy Spirit at Pentecost, Peter, taking the lead among the assembly of believers in Jerusalem, stood up and announced the essential qualification. Two names met this essential and of these one was chosen, Matthias. This man knew the historical Jesus before the resurrection, he had kept company with him throughout the whole of the ministry. He had seen it all. He knew as far as any man is able to know what Jesus was like. Without that qualification he could not be an apostle and without the apostles there can be no Christian Church.

2 READING THE HISTORY WITH FAITH

No, we cannot sit lightly to the historical Jesus in our Christian discipleship. We must keep company with him as he was *and is*. And now I have gone beyond history. I am referring to him as the risen Jesus. He is that for us in the Christian Church. We look back therefore at the historical Jesus with the eyes of this faith and so he speaks to us today through these vivid stories in the various situations in which we find ourselves.

Let me end with a story, a true one, taken from modern life. A child ran out of the house to greet her father coming home. There was a screech of brakes from an oncoming car. He hurried to pick up her crumpled form. She was dead. The local clergyman called at the house but was so overcome by the brokenness of the family, not least the father who had carried the child back into the house, that he could think of no appropriate words of comfort. He had however a Bible in his pocket and opening it his eye lit on the story of Jesus entering the room where the daughter of a synagogue president lay dead on a bed. In the story all were distraught at this pathetic sight. But Jesus quietened the scene and said 'The girl is not dead, she is asleep'. The clergyman read the passage of Scripture out loud. When he reached the words 'The girl is not dead, she is asleep' the father stopped him. 'Will you read that at the funeral, then I think I can go through with it?' And he did. This story of the historical Jesus became much more than an historical record that day. This is how the stories in the gospels are read in the Christian Church. They are read with the eyes of faith in *the risen Christ*. Then they convey a *contemporary* message. This is how they came to be written down in the first place. This is why they are not outdated even after the passage of nearly two thousand years. They come alive.